ISBN 978-1-332-43245-5
PIBN 10426132

1 MONTH OF
FREE
READING

at

www.ForgottenBooks.com

By purchasing this book you are eligible for one month membership to ForgottenBooks.com, giving you unlimited access to our entire collection of over 700,000 titles via our web site and mobile apps.

To claim your free month visit:

www.forgottenbooks.com/free426132

English
Français
Deutsche
Italiano
Español
Português

www.forgottenbooks.com

Mythology Photography **Fiction**
Fishing Christianity **Art** Cooking
Essays Buddhism Freemasonry
Medicine **Biology** Music **Ancient
Egypt** Evolution Carpentry Physics
Dance Geology **Mathematics** Fitness
Shakespeare **Folklore** Yoga Marketing
Confidence Immortality Biographies
Poetry **Psychology** Witchcraft
Electronics Chemistry History **Law**
Accounting **Philosophy** Anthropology
Alchemy Drama Quantum Mechanics
Atheism Sexual Health **Ancient History**
Entrepreneurship Languages Sport
Paleontology Needlework Islam
Metaphysics Investment Archaeology
Parenting Statistics Criminology
Motivational

HE LOST GOSPEL AND ITS CONTENTS;

OR,

HE AUTHOR OF "SUPERNATURAL RELIGION"

REFUTED BY HIMSELF.

BY THE REV. M. F. SADLER, M.A.,

RECTOR OF HONITON.

LONDON:

GEORGE BELL AND SONS, YORK STREET,

COVENT GARDEN.

1876.

CHISWICK PRESS.—PRINTED BY WHITTINGHAM AND WILKINS,
TOOKS COURT, CHANCERY LANE.

PREFACE.

THIS book is entitled "The Lost Gospel," because the book to which it is an answer is an attempt to discredit the Supernatural element of Christianity by undermining the authority of our present Gospels in favour of an earlier form of the narrative which has perished.

It seemed to me that, if the author of "Supernatural Religion" proved his point, and demonstrated that the Fathers of the Second Century quoted Gospels earlier than those which we now possess, then the evidence for the Supernatural itself, considered as apart from the particular books in which the records of it are contained, would be strengthened; if, that is, it could be .shown that this earlier form of the narrative contained the same Supernatural Story.

The author of "Supernatural Religion," whilst he has utterly failed to show that the Fathers in question have used earlier Gospels, has, to my mind, proved to demonstration that, if they have quoted earlier narratives, those accounts contain, not only substantially, but in detail, the same Gospel which we now possess, and in a form rather more suggestive of the Supernatural. So that, if he has been successful, the author has only succeeded in proving that the Gospel narrative itself, in a written form, is at least fifty or sixty years older than the books which he attempts to discredit.

With respect to Justin Martyr, to the bearing of whose writings on this subject I have devoted the greater part of my book, I can only say that, in my examination of his works, my bias was with the author of " Supernatural Religion." I had hitherto believed that this Father, being a native of Palestine, and living so near to the time of the Apostles, was acquainted with views of certain great truths which he had derived from traditions of the oral teaching of the Apostles, and the possession of which made him in some measure an independent witness for the views in question; but I confess that, on a closer examination of his writings, I was somewhat disappointed, for I found that he had no knowledge of our Lord and of His teaching worth speaking of, except what he might be fairly assumed to have derived from our present New Testament.

I have to acknowledge my obligations to Messrs. Clark, of Edinburgh, for allowing me to make somewhat copious extracts from the writings of Justin in their ante-Nicene Library. This has saved a Parish Priest like myself much time and trouble. I believe that in all cases of importance in which I have altered the translation, or felt that there was a doubt, I have given the original from Otto's edition (Jena, 1842).

CONTENTS.

PAGE

INTRODUCTORY.

IN the following pages I have examined the conclusions at which the author of a book entitled "Supernatural Religion" has assumed to have arrived.

The method and contents of the work in question may be thus described.

The work is entitled "Supernatural Religion, an Inquiry into the Reality of Divine Revelation." Its contents occupy two volumes of about 500 pages each, so that we have in it an elaborate attack upon Christianity of very considerable length. The first 200 pages of the first volume are filled with arguments to prove that a Revelation, such as the one we profess to believe in, supernatural in its origin and nature and attested by miracles, is simply incredible, and so, on no account, no matter how evidenced, to be received.

But, inasmuch as the author has to face the fact, that the Christian Religion professes to be attested by miracles performed at a very late period in the history of the

world, and said to have been witnessed by very large
numbers of persons, and related very fully in certain
books called the Canonical Gospels, which the whole
body of Christians have, from a very early period indeed,
received as written by eye-witnesses, or by the companions of eye-witnesses, the remaining 800 pages are
occupied with attempts at disparaging the testimony
of these writings. In order to this, the Christian
Fathers and heretical writers of a certain period are
examined, to ascertain whether they quoted the four
Evangelists. The period from which the writer chooses
his witnesses to the use of the four Evangelists, is most
unwarrantably and arbitrarily restricted to the first ninety
years of the second century (100—185 or so). We shall
have ample means for showing that this limitation was
for a purpose.

The array of witnesses examined runs thus : Clement
of Rome, Barnabas, Hermas, Ignatius, Polycarp, Justin
Martyr, Hegesippus, Papias of Hierapolis, the Clemen-
tines, the Epistle to Diognetus, Basilides, Valentinus,
Marcion, Tatian, Dionysius of Corinth, Melito of Sardis,
Claudius Apollinaris, Athenagoras, Epistle of Vienne and
Lyons, Ptolemæus and Heracleon, Celsus and the Canon
of Muratori.

The examination of references, or supposed references,
in these books to the first three Gospels fills above 500
pages, and the remainder (about 220) is occupied with
an examination of the claims of the fourth Gospel to be
considered as canonical.

The writer conducts this examination with an avowed
dogmatical bias ; and this, as the reader will soon see,
influences the manner of his examination throughout the

whole book. For instance, he never fails to give to the anti-Christian side the benefit of every doubt, or even suspicion. This leads him to make the most of the smallest discrepancy between the words of any supposed quotation in any early writer from one of our Canonical Gospels, and the words as contained in our present Gospels. If the writer quotes the Evangelist freely, with some differences, however slight, in the words, he is assumed to quote from a lost Apocryphal Gospel. If the writer gives the words as we find them in our Gospels, he attempts to show that the father or heretic need not have even seen our present Gospels; for, inasmuch as our present Gospels have many things in common which are derived from an earlier source, the quoter may have derived the words he quotes from the earlier source. If the quoter actually mentions the name of the Evangelist whose Gospel he refers to (say St. Mark), it is roundly asserted that his St. Mark is not the same as ours.[1]

The reader may ask, "How is it possible, against such a mode of argument, to prove the genuineness or authenticity of any book, sacred or profane?" And, of course, it is not. Such a way of conducting a controversy seems absurd, but on the author's premises it is a necessity. He asserts the dogma that the Governor of the world cannot interfere by way of miracle. He has to meet the fact that the foremost religion of the world appeals to miracles, especially the miracle of the Resurrection of

---

[1] Papias, for instance, actually mentions St. Mark by name as writing a gospel under the influence of St. Peter. The author of "Supernatural Religion" devotes ten pages to an attempt to prove that this St. Mark's Gospel could not be ours. (Vol. i. pp. 448-459.)

the Founder. For the truth of this miraculous Resurrection there is at least a thousand times more evidence than there is for any historical fact which is recorded to have occurred 1,800 years ago. Of course, if the supernatural in Christianity is impossible, and so incredible, all the witnesses to it must be discredited; and their number, their age, and their unanimity upon the principal points are such that the mere attempt must tax the powers of human labour and ingenuity to the uttermost.

How, then, is such a book to be met? It would take a work of twice the size to rebut all the assertions of the author, for, naturally, an answer to any assertion must take up more space than the assertion. Fortunately, in this case, we are not driven to any such course; for, as I shall show over and over again, the author has furnished us with the most ample means for his own refutation. No book that I have ever read or heard of contains so much which can be met by implication from the pages of the author himself, nor can I imagine any book of such pretensions pervaded with so entire a misconception of the conditions of the problem on which he is writing.

These assertions I shall now, God helping, proceed to make good.

THE WAY CLEARED.

THE writers, whose testimonies to the existence or use of our present Gospels are examined by the author, are twenty-three in number. Five of these, namely, Hegesippus, Papias, Melito, Claudius Apollinaris, and Dionysius of Corinth are only known to us through fragments preserved as quotations in Eusebius and others. Six others—Basilides, Valentinus, Marcion, Ptolemæus, Heracleon, and Celsus—are heretical or infidel writers, whom we only know through notices or scraps of their works in the writings of the Christian Fathers who refuted them. The Epistle of the Martyrs of Vienne and Lyons is only in part preserved in the pages of Eusebius. The Canon of Muratori is a mutilated fragment of uncertain date. Athenagoras and Tatian are only known through Apologies written for the Heathen, the last of all Christian books in which to look for definite references to canonical writings. The Epistle to Diognetus is a small tract of uncertain date and authorship. The Clementine Homilies is an apocryphal work of very little value in the present discussion.

These are all the writings placed by the author as subsequent to Justin Martyr. The writers previous to

Justin, of whom the author of "Supernatural Religion" makes use, are Clement of Rome (to whom we shall afterwards refer), the Epistle of Barnabas, the Pastor of Hermas, the Epistles of Ignatius, and that of Polycarp.

As I desire to take the author on his own ground whenever it is possible to do so, I shall, for argument's sake, take the author's account of the age and authority of these documents. I shall consequently assume with him that

"None of the epistles [of Ignatius] have any value as evidence for an earlier period than the end of the second or beginning of the third century [from about 190 to 210 or so], if indeed they possess any value at all."[1] (Vol. i. p. 274.)

With respect to the short Epistle of Polycarp, I shall be patient of his assumption that

"Instead of proving the existence of the epistles of Ignatius, with which it is intimately associated, it is itself discredited in proportion as they are shown to be inauthentic." (Vol. i. p. 274.)

---

[1] I need hardly say that I myself hold the genuineness of the Greek recension. The reader who desires to see the false reasonings and groundless assumptions of the author of "Supernatural Religion" respecting the Ignatian epistles thoroughly exposed should read Professor Lightfoot's article in the "Contemporary Review" of February, 1875. In pages 341-345 of this article there is an examination of the nature and trustworthiness of the learning displayed in the footnotes of this pretentious book, which is particularly valuable. I am glad to see that the professor has modified, in this article, the expression of his former opinion that the excerpta called the Curetonian recension is to be regarded as the only genuine one. "Elsewhere," the professor writes (referring to an essay in his commentary on the Philippians), "I had acquiesced in the earlier opinion of Lipsius, who ascribed them (*i. e.*, the Greek or Vossian recension) to an interpolator writing about A.D. 140. Now, however, I am obliged to confess that I have grave and increasing doubts whether, after all, they are not the genuine utterances of Ignatius himself."

and so he

" assigns it to the latter half of the second century, in so far as any genuine part of it is concerned." (P. 275.)

Similarly, I shall assume that the Pastor of Hermas "may have been written about the middle of the second century" (p. 256), and, with respect to the Epistle of Barnabas, I shall take the latest date mentioned by the author of "Supernatural Religion," where he writes respecting the epistle:—

" There is little or no certainty how far into the second century its composition may not reasonably be advanced. Critics are divided upon the point; a few are disposed to date the epistle about the end of the first century; others at the beginning of the second century; while a still greater number assign it to the reign of Adrian (A.D. 117-130); and others, not without reason, consider that it exhibits marks of a still later period." (Vol. i. p. 235.)

The way, then, is so far cleared that I can confine my remarks to the investigation of the supposed citations from the Canonical Gospels, to be found in the works of Justin Martyr. Before beginning this, it may be well to direct the reader's attention to the real point at issue; and this I shall have to do continually throughout my examination. The work is entitled " Supernatural Religion," and is an attack upon what the author calls " Ecclesiastical Christianity," because such Christianity sets forth the Founder of our Religion as conceived and born in a supernatural way; as doing throughout His life supernatural acts; as dying for a supernatural purpose; and as raised from the dead by a miracle, which was the sign and seal of the truth of all His supernatural claims. The attack in the book in question takes the form of a continuous effort to show that all our four Gospels are unauthentic, by showing, or attempting to show, that they were never quoted before the latter part of the second century: but the real point of attack is the supernatural in the records of Christ's Birth, Life, Death, and Resurrection.

THE PRINCIPAL WITNESS.—HIS RELIGIOUS VIEWS.

THE examination of the quotations in Justin Martyr of the Synoptic Gospels occupies nearly one hundred and fifty pages; and deservedly so, for the acknowledged writings of this Father are, if we except the Clementine forgeries and the wild vision of Hermas, more in length than those of all the other twenty-three witnesses put together. They are also valuable because no doubts can be thrown upon their date, and because they take up, or advert to, so many subjects of interest to Christians in all ages.

The universally acknowledged writings of Justin Martyr are three:—Two Apologies addressed to the Heathen, and a Dialogue with Trypho a Jew.

The first Apology is addressed to the Emperor Antoninus Pius, and was written before the year 150 A.D. The second Apology is by some supposed to be the first in point of publication, and is addressed to the Roman people.

The contents of the two Apologies are remarkable in this respect, that Justin scruples not to bring before the heathen the very arcana of Christianity. No apologist shows so little " reserve" in stating to the heathen the mysteries of the faith. At the very outset he enunciates the doctrine of the Incarnate Logos:—

" For not only among the Greeks did Logos (or Reason) prevail to condemn these things by Socrates, but also among the barbarians were they condemned by the Logos himself, who took shape and became man, and was called Jesus Christ."[1]　(Apol. i. 5.)

In the next chapter he sets forth the doctrine and worship of the Trinity :—

" But both Him [the Father] and the Son, Who came forth from Him and taught these things to us and the host of heaven, the other good angels who follow and are made like to Him, and the Prophetic Spirit, we worship and adore, knowing them in reason and truth." [2]

Again :—

" Our teacher of these things is Jesus Christ, Who was also born for this purpose, and was crucified under Pontius Pilate, procurator of Judæa, in the time of Tiberius Cæsar; and that we reasonably worship Him, having learned that He is the Son of the True God Himself, and holding Him in the second place, and the Prophetic Spirit in the third." (Apol. i. ch. x. 3.)

Again, a little further on, he claims for Christians a higher belief in the supernatural than the heathen had, for, whereas the heathen went no further than believing that souls after death are in a state of sensation, Christians believed in the resurrection of the body :—

---

[1] Οὐ γὰρ μόνον ἐν Ἕλλησι διὰ Σωκράτους ὑπὸ λόγου ἠλέγχθη ταῦτα, ἀλλὰ καὶ ἐν βαρβάροις ὑπ᾽ αὐτοῦ τοῦ Λόγου μορφωθέντος καὶ ἀνθρώπου γενομένου καὶ Ἰησοῦ Χριστοῦ κληθέντος.

[2] Such is a perfectly allowable translation of καὶ τὸν παρ᾽ αὐτοῦ υἱὸν ἐλθόντα καὶ διδάξαντα ἡμᾶς ταῦτα, καὶ τὸν τῶν ἄλλων ἑπομένων καὶ ἐξομοιουμένων ἀγαθῶν ἀγγέλων στρατόν, πνεῦμά τε τὸ προφητικὸν σεβόμεθα καὶ προσκυνοῦμεν. As there is nothing approaching to angel worship in Justin, such a rendering seems absolutely necessary.

"Such favour as you grant to these, grant also unto us, who not less but more firmly than they believe in God; since we expect to receive again our own bodies, though they be dead and cast into the earth, for we maintain that with God nothing is impossible." (Apol. I. ch. xviii.)

In the next chapter (xix.) he proceeds to prove the Resurrection possible. This he does from the analogy of human generation, and he concludes thus :—

" So also judge ye that it is not impossible that the bodies of men after they have been dissolved, and like seeds resolved into earth, should in God's appointed time rise again and put on incorruption."

In another place in the same Apology he asserts the personality of Satan :—

" For among us the prince of the wicked spirits is called the serpent, and Satan, and the devil, as you can learn by looking into our writings, and that he would be sent into the fire with his host, and the men who followed him, and would be punished for an endless duration, Christ foretold." (Apol. I. ch. xxviii.)

In the same short chapter he asserts in very weighty words his belief in the ever-watchful providence of God :—

" And if any one disbelieves that God cares for these things (the welfare of the human race), he will thereby either insinuate that God does not exist, or he will assert that though He exists He delights in vice, or exists like a stone, and that neither virtue nor vice are anything, but only in the opinion of men these things are reckoned good or evil, and this is the greatest profanity and wickedness." (Apol. I. ch. xxviii.)

Shortly after this he tells the heathen Emperor that the mission and work of Jesus Christ had been predicted:—

" There were amongst the Jews certain men who were prophets of God, through whom the Prophetic Spirit published
beforehand things that were to come to pass, ere ever they
happened. And their prophecies, as they were spoken and
when they were uttered, the kings who happened to be
reigning among the Jews at the several times carefully preserved in their possession, when they had been arranged
in books by the prophets themselves in their own Hebrew
language. . . . . In these books, then, of the prophets, we
found Jesus Christ foretold as coming, born of a virgin, growing up to man's estate, and healing every disease and every
sickness, and raising the dead, and being hated, and unre-
cognized, and crucified, and dying and rising again, and ascending into heaven, and being, and being called, the Son of God.
We find it also predicted that certain persons should be sent
by Him into every nation to publish these things, and that
rather among the Gentiles (than among the Jews) men should
believe on Him. And He was predicted before He appeared,
first 5,000 years before, and again 3,000, then 2,000, then
1,000, and yet again 800; for in the succession of generations
prophets after prophets arose."   (Apol. i. ch. xxxi.)

Then he proceeds to show how certain particular prophecies which he cites were fulfilled in the Jews having
a lawgiver till the time of Christ, and not after; in
Christ's entry into Jerusalem ; in His Birth of a Virgin ;
in the place of His Birth; in His having His hands and
feet pierced with the nails. (Ch. xxxiii., xxxiv., xxxv.)

Again, immediately afterwards, he endeavours to
classify certain prophecies as peculiarly those of God the
Father, certain others as peculiarly those of God the
Son, and others as the special utterance of the Spirit.
(Ch. xxxvi.-xl.)

Then he proceeds to specify certain particular prophecies as fulfilled in our Lord's Advent (ch. xl.) ;

certain others in His Crucifixion (xli.); in His Session in heaven (xlv.); in the desolation of Judæa (xlvii.); in the miracles and Death of Christ (xlviii.); in His rejection by the Jews (xlix.); in His Humiliation (l.) He concludes with asserting the extreme importance of prophecy, as without it we should not be warranted in believing such things of any one of the human race :—

"For with what reason should we believe of a crucified Man that He is the first-born of the unbegotten God, and Himself will pass judgment on the whole human race, unless we have found testimonies concerning Him published before He came, and was born as man, and unless we saw that things had happened accordingly,—the devastation of the land of the Jews, and men of every race persuaded by His teaching through the Apostles, and rejecting their old habits, in which, being deceived, they had had their conversation." (Ch. liii.)

After this he speaks (ch. lxi.) of Christian Baptism, as being in some sense a conveyance of Regeneration, and of the Eucharist (ch. lxvi.), as being a mysterious communication of the Flesh and Blood of Christ, and at the conclusion he describes the worship of Christians, and tells the Emperor that in their assemblies the memoirs of the Apostles (by which name he designates the accounts of the Birth, Life, and Death of Christ), or the writings of the Prophets were read, as long as time permits, putting the former on a par with the latter, as equally necessary for the instruction of Christians.

Besides this, we find that Justin holds all these views of Scripture truths which are now called Evangelical. He speaks of men now being

" Purified no longer by the blood of goats and sheep, or by

the ashes of an heifer, or by the offerings of fine flour, but by faith through the Blood of Christ, and through His Death, Who died for this very reason." (Dial.)

And again:

"So that it becomes you to eradicate this hope (*i.e.* of salvation by Jewish ordinances) from your souls, and hasten to know in what way forgiveness of sins, and a hope of inheriting the promised good things, shall be yours. But there is no other way than this to become acquainted with this Christ, to be washed in the fountain spoken of by Isaiah for the remission of sins, and for the rest to lead sinless lives." (Dial. xliv.)

So that from this Apology alone, though addressed to the heathen, we learn that Justin cordially accepted every supernatural element in Christianity. He thoroughly believed in the Trinity, the Incarnation of the Logos, the miraculous Conception, Birth, Life, Miracles, Death, Resurrection, and Ascension of Christ. He firmly believed in the predictive element in prophecy, in the atoning virtue of the Death of Christ, in the mysterious inward grace or inward part in each Sacrament, in the heart-cleansing power of the Spirit of God, in the particular providence of God, in the resurrection of the body, in eternal reward and eternal punishment.

Whatever, then, was the source of his knowledge, that knowledge made him intensely dogmatic in his creed, and a firm believer in the supernatural nature of everything in his religion.

The Second Apology is of the same nature as the first. A single short extract or two from it will show how firmly the author held the supernatural:—

"Our doctrines, then, appear to be greater than all human teaching; because Christ, who appeared for our sakes, became the whole rational being, both body, and reason, and soul. . . . . These things our Christ did through His own power. For no one trusted in Socrates so as to die for this doctrine; but in Christ, who was partially known even by Socrates (for He was and is the Word Who is in every man, and Who foretold the things that were to come to pass both through the prophets and in His own Person when He was made of like passions, and taught these things); not only philosophers and scholars believed, but also artizans and people entirely uneducated, despising both glory, and fear, and death; since He is a Power of the ineffable Father, and not the mere instrument of human reason." (Apol. II. ch. x.)

The dialogue with Trypho is the record of a lengthy discussion with a Jew for the purpose of converting him to the Christian faith. The assertion of the supernatural is here, if possible, more unreserved than in the First Apology. In order to convert Trypho, Justin cites every prophecy of the Old Testament that can, with the smallest show of reason, be referred to Christ.

Having, first of all, vindicated the Christians from the charge of setting aside the Jewish law or covenant, by an argument evidently derived from the Epistle to the Hebrews,[1] and vindicated for Christians the title of the true spiritual Israel,[2] he proceeds to the prophetical

---

[1] "For the law promulgated in Horeb is now old, and belongs to you alone; but this is for all universally. Now law placed against law has abrogated that which is before it, and a covenant which comes after in like manner has put an end to the previous one; and an eternal and final law—namely, Christ—has been given to us." (Heb. viii. 6-13; Dial. ch. xi.)

[2] "For the true spiritual Israel and descendants of Judah, Jacob, Isaac, and Abraham (who in uncircumcision was approved of and blessed by God on account of his faith, and called the father of many nations) are we who have been led to God through this crucified Christ, as shall be demonstrated while we proceed." (Phil. iii. 3, compared with Romans, iv. 12-18; Dial. ch. xi.)

Scriptures, and transcribes the whole of the prophecy of Isaiah from the fifty-second chapter to the fifty-fourth, and applies it to Christ and His Kingdom. (Dial. ch. xiii.) Shortly after, he applies to the second Advent of Christ the prophecy of Daniel respecting the Son of Man, brought before the Ancient of Days. (Ch. xxxi.) Then he notices and refutes certain destructive interpretations of prophecies which have been derived from the unbelieving Jews by our modern rationalists, as that Psalm cx. is spoken of Hezekiah, and Psalm lxxii. of Solomon.

Then he proceeds to prove that Christ is both God and Lord of Hosts; and he first cites Psalm xxiv., and then Psalms xlvi., xcviii., and xlv. (Ch. xxxvi., xxxvii., xxxviii.)

Then, after returning to the Mosaic law, and proving that certain points in its ritual were fulfilled in the Christian system (as the oblation of fine flour in the Eucharist—ch. xli.), he concludes this part of his argument with the assertion that the Mosaic law had an end in Christ —

"In short, sirs," said I, "by enumerating all the other appointments of Moses, I can demonstrate that they were types, and symbols, and declarations of those things which would happen to Christ, of those who, it was foreknown, were to believe in Him, and of those things which would also be done by Christ Himself." (Ch. xlii.)

Then he again proves that this Christ was to be, and was, born of a virgin; and takes occasion to show that the virgin mentioned in Isaiah vii. was not a young married woman, as rationalists in Germany and among ourselves have learnt from the unbelieving Jews. (Ch. xliii.)

To go over more of Justin's argument would be beside my purpose, which is at present simply to show how very firmly his faith embraced the supernatural.

I shall mention one more application of prophecy. When Trypho asks that Justin should resume the discourse, and show that the Spirit of prophecy admits another God besides the Maker of all things,[1] Justin accepts his challenge, and commences with the appearance of the three angels to Abraham, and devotes much space and labour to a sifting discussion of the meaning of this place. The conclusion is thus expressed :—

" And now have you not perceived, my friends, that one of the three, Who is both God and Lord, and ministers to Him Who is [remains] in the heavens, is Lord of the two angels ? For when [the angels] proceeded to Sodom He remained behind, and communed with Abraham in the words recorded by Moses ; and when He departed after the conversation Abraham went back to his place. And when He came [to Sodom] the two angels no longer converse with Lot, but Himself, as the Scripture makes evident; and He is the Lord Who received commission from the Lord Who [remains] in the heavens, i. e. the Maker of all things, to inflict upon Sodom and Gomorrah the [judgments] which the Scripture describes in these terms: 'The Lord rained upon Sodom sulphur and fire from the Lord out of heaven.' " (Ch. lvi.)

It is clear from all this that Justin Martyr looked upon prophecy as a supernatural gift, bestowed upon men in order to prepare them to receive that Christ whom God would send. Instead of regarding it as the natural surmising of far-seeing men who, from their experience

---

[1] This, of course, was a Jewish adversary's view of the Christian doctrine of the Godhead of Christ, which Justin elsewhere modifies by showing the subordination of the Son to the Father in all things.

of the past, and from their knowledge of human nature, could in some sort guess what course events are likely to take, he regarded it as a Divine influence emanating from Him Who knows the future as perfectly as He knows the past, and for His own purposes revealing events, and in many cases what we should call *trifling* events, which would be wholly out of the power of man to guess or even to imagine.

I am not, of course, concerned to show that Justin was right in his views of prophecy; all I am concerned to show is, that Justin regarded prophecy as the highest of supernatural gifts.

Such, then, was the view of Justin respecting Christ and the Religion He established. Christ, the highest of supernatural beings, His Advent foretold by men with supernatural gifts to make known the future, coming to us in the highest of supernatural ways, and establishing a supernatural kingdom for bringing about such supernatural ends as the reconciliation of all men to God by His Sacrifice, the Resurrection of the body, and the subjugation of the wills of all men to the Will of God.

THE PRINCIPAL WITNESS.—THE SOURCES OF HIS
KNOWLEDGE RESPECTING THE
BIRTH OF CHRIST.

THE question now arises, and I beg the reader to remember that it is the question on which the author of "Supernatural Religion" stakes all,—From what source did Justin derive this supernatural view of Christianity?

With respect to the Incarnation, Birth, Life, Death, and Resurrection of Christ, he evidently derives it from certain documents which he repeatedly cites, as " The Memoirs of the Apostles" ('Απομνημονεύματα τῶν 'Αποστό-λων). These are the documents which he mentions as being read, along with the Prophets, at the meetings of Christians.

On one occasion, when he is seemingly referring to the [bloody] sweat of our Lord, which is mentioned only in St. Luke, who is not an Apostle, he designates these writings as the " Memoirs which were drawn up by the Apostles *and those who followed them.*"[1] Again, on another occasion, he seems to indicate specially the Gospel of St. Mark as being the " Memoirs of Peter." It is a

---

[1] 'Εν γὰρ τοῖς ἀπομνημονεύμασι, ἅ φημι ὑπὸ τῶν ἀποστόλων αὐτοῦ καὶ τῶν ἐκείνοις παρακολουθησάντων συντετάχθαι, ὅτι ἰδρὼς ὡσεὶ θρόμβοι κατεχεῖτο αὐτοῦ εὐχομένου. (Dial. ch. ciii.)

well-known fact that all ecclesiastical tradition, almost with one voice, has handed down that St. Mark wrote his Gospel under the superintendence, if not at the dictation, of St. Peter; and when Justin has occasion to mention that our Lord gave the name of Boanerges to the sons of Zebedee, an incident mentioned only by St. Mark, he seems at least to indicate the Gospel of St. Mark as being specially connected with St. Peter as his Memoirs when he writes :[1]—

"And when it is said that he changed the name of one of the Apostles to Peter; and when it is written in his Memoirs that this so happened, as well as that He changed the names of two other brothers, the sons of Zebedee, to Boanerges, which means 'sons of thunder;' this was an announcement," &c. (Ch. cvi.)

With the exception of these two apparent cases, Justin never distinguishes one Memoir from another. He never mentions the author or authors of the Memoirs by name, and for this reason—that the three undoubted treatises of his which have come down to us are all written for those outside the pale of the Christian Church. It would have been worse than useless, in writing for such persons, to distinguish between Evangelist and Evangelist. So far as "those without" were concerned, the Evangelists

---

[1] Καὶ τὸ εἰπεῖν μετωνομακέναι αὐτὸν Πέτρον ἕνα τῶν ἀποστόλων, καὶ γεγράφθαι ἐν τοῖς ἀπομνημονεύμασιν αὐτοῦ γεγενημένον καὶ τοῦτο, κ. τ. λ.

On this quotation the author of "Supernatural Religion" remarks, "According to the usual language of Justin, and upon strictly critical grounds, the αὐτοῦ in this passage must be ascribed to Peter; and Justin therefore seems to ascribe the Memoirs to that Apostle, and to speak consequently of a Gospel of Peter." (Vol. i. p. 417.)

gave the same view of Christ and His work; and to have quoted first one and then another by name would have been mischievous, as indicating differences when the testimony of all that could be called memoirs was, in point of fact, one and the same.

According to the author of " Supernatural Religion " Justin ten times designates the source of his quotations as the " Memoirs of the Apostles," and five times as simply the " Memoirs."

Now the issue which the writer of " Supernatural Religion " raises is this: " Were these Memoirs our present four Gospels, or were they some older Gospel or Gospels ?" to which we may add another : " Did Justin quote any other lost Gospel besides our four? "

I shall now give some instances of the use which Justin makes of the writings which he calls " Memoirs," and this will enable the reader in great measure to judge for himself.

First of all, then, I give one or two extracts from Justin's account of our Lord's Nativity. Let the reader remember that, with respect to the first of these, the account is not introduced in order to give Trypho an account of our Lord's Birth, but to assure him that a certain prophecy, as it is worded in the Septuagint translation of Isaiah—viz., " He shall take the powers of Damascus and the spoil of Samaria," was fulfilled in Christ. And indeed almost every incident which Justin takes notice of he relates as a fulfilment of some prophecy or other. Trifling or comparatively trifling incidents in our Lord's Life are noticed at great length, because they are supposed to be the fulfilment of some prophecy; and what we should consider more important events are passed over in silence, because they do not seem to fulfil any prediction.

The first extract from Justin, then, shall be the following :—

"Now this King Herod, at the time when the Magi came to him from Arabia, and said they knew from a star which appeared in the heavens that a King had been born in your country, and that they had come to worship Him, learned from the Elders of your people, that it was thus written regarding Bethlehem in the Prophet: 'And thou, Bethlehem, in the land of Judah, art by no means least among the princes of Judah; for out of thee shall go forth the leader, who shall feed my people.' Accordingly, the Magi from Arabia came to Bethlehem, and worshipped the child, and presented him with gifts, gold, and frankincense, and myrrh; but returned not to Herod, being warned in a revelation after worshipping the child in Bethlehem. And Joseph, the spouse of Mary, who wished at first to put away his betrothed Mary, supposing her to be pregnant by intercourse with a man, *i. e.* from fornication, was commanded in a vision not to put away his wife; and the angel who appeared to him told him that what is in her womb is of the Holy Ghost. Then he was afraid and did not put her away, but on the occasion of the first census which was taken in Judea under Cyrenius, he went up from Nazareth, where he lived, to Bethlehem, to which he belonged, to be enrolled; for his family was of the tribe of Judah, which then inhabited that region. Then, along with Mary, he is ordered to proceed into Egypt, and remain there with the Child, until another revelation warn them to return to Judea. But when the Child was born in Bethlehem, since Joseph could not find a lodging in that village, he took up his quarters in a certain cave near the village; and while they were there Mary brought forth the Christ and placed Him in a manger, and here the Magi who came from Arabia found Him. 'I have repeated to you,' I continued, 'what

Isaiah foretold about the sign which foreshadowed the cave; but, for the sake of those which have come with us to-day, I shall again remind you of the passage.' Then I repeated the passage from Isaiah which I have already written, adding that, by means of those words, those who presided over the mysteries of Mithras were stirred up by the devil to say that in a place, called among them a cave, they were initiated by him. 'So Herod, when the Magi from Arabia did not return to him, as he had asked them to do, but had departed by another way to their own country, according to the commands laid upon them; and when Joseph, with Mary and the Child, had now gone into Egypt, as it was revealed to them to do; as he did not know the Child whom the Magi had gone to worship, ordered simply the whole of the children then in Bethlehem to be massacred. And Jeremiah prophesied that this would happen, speaking by the Holy Ghost thus: 'A voice was heard in Ramah, lamentation and much wailing, Rachel weeping for her children, and she would not be comforted, because they are not.'" (Dial. ch. lxxviii.)

Now any unprejudiced reader, on examining this account, would instantly say that Justin had derived every word of it from the Gospels of St. Matthew and St. Luke, but that, instead of quoting the exact words of either Evangelist, he would say that he (Justin) "reproduced" them. He reproduced the narrative of the Nativity as it is found in each of these two Gospels. He first reproduces the narrative in St. Matthew in somewhat more colloquial phrase than the Evangelist used, interspersing with it remarks of his own; and in order to account for the Birth of Christ in Bethlehem he brings in from St. Luke the matter of the census, (not with historical accuracy but) sufficiently to show that he was acquainted with the beginning of Luke ii.; and in order to account for the fact that Christ was not

born in the inn, but in a more sordid place (whether
stable or cave matters not, for if it was a cave it was a
cave used as a stable, for there was a "manger" in it),
he reproduces Luke ii. 6-7.

Justin then, in a single consecutive narrative, expressed much in his own words, gives the whole account,
so far as it was a fulfilment of prophecy, made up from
two narratives which have come down to us in the
Gospels of St. Matthew and St. Luke, and in these
only. It would have been absurd for him to have done
otherwise, as he might have done if he had anticipated
the carpings of nineteenth century critics, and assumed
that Trypho, an unconverted Jew, had a New Testament
in his hand with which he was so familiar that he could
be referred to first one narrative and then the other, in
order to test the correctness of Justin's quotations.

Against all this the author of "Supernatural Religion"
brings forward a number of trifling disagreements as
proofs that Justin need not have quoted one of the
Evangelists—probably did not—indeed, may not have
ever seen our synoptics, or heard of their existence.
But the reader will observe that he has given the same
history as we find in the two synoptics which have
given an account of the Nativity, and he apparently
knew of no other account of the matter.

We are reminded that there were numerous apocryphal Gospels then in use in the Church, and that
Justin might have derived his matter from these; but, if
so, how is it that he discards all the lying legends with
which those Gospels team, and, with the solitary exception of the mention of the cave, confines himself to
the circumstances of the synoptic narrative.

The next place respecting the Nativity shall be one from ch. c. :—

" But the Virgin Mary received faith and joy, when the angel Gabriel announced the good tidings to her that the Spirit of the Lord would come upon her, and the power of the Highest would overshadow her ; wherefore also the Holy Thing begotten of her is the Son of God : and she replied, ' Be it unto me according to Thy word.' "

Here both the words of the angel and the answer of the virgin are almost identical with the words in St. Luke's Gospel; Justin, however, putting his account into the oblique narrative.

We will put the two side by side that the reader may compare them.

Πίστιν δὲ καὶ χαρὰν λαβοῦσα Μαρία ἡ παρθένος εὐαγγελιζομένου αὐτῇ Γαβριὴλ ἀγγέλου, ὅτι πνεῦμα κυρίου ἐπ' αὐτὴν ἐπελεύσεται, καὶ δύναμις ὑψίστου ἐπισκιάσει αὐτὴν, διὸ καὶ τὸ γεννώμενον ἐξ αὐτῆς ἅγιόν ἐστιν Υἱὸς Θεοῦ, ἀπεκρίνατο, Γένοιτό μοι κατὰ τὸ ῥῆμά σου.

Πνεῦμα ἅγιον ἐπελεύσεται ἐπί σέ, καὶ δύναμις ὑψίστου ἐπισκιάσει σοι, διὸ καὶ τὸ γεννώμενον ἅγιον κληθήσεται Υἱὸς Θεοῦ.

. . . . .

Γένοιτό μοι κατὰ τὸ ῥῆμά σου.

Now of these words, *as existing in St. Luke,* the author of " Supernatural Religion " takes no notice. Was he, then, acquainted with the fact that Justin's words *in this place* so closely correspond with St. Luke's? We cannot say. We only know that he calls his readers' particular attention to a supposed citation of the previous words of the angel Gabriel, cited in another place :—

" Behold thou shalt conceive of the Holy Ghost, and shalt bear a Son, and He shall be called the Son of the Highest, and thou shalt call His name Jesus, for He shall save His people from their sins." (Apol. 1, ch. xxxiii.)

The ordinary unprejudiced reader would say that Justin here reproduces St. Matthew and St. Luke, weaving into St. Luke's narrative the words of the angel to St. Joseph; but our author will not allow this for a moment. He insists that Justin knew nothing, or need have known nothing, of St. Luke. He shows that the words of the angel, "He shall save his people," &c., which seem to be introduced from St. Matthew, "are not accidentally inserted in this place, for we find that they are joined in the same manner to the address of the angel to Mary in the Protevangelium of St. James."

But how about those words which succeed them in answer to the question of the Virgin, "How shall these things be?" I mean those quoted in the "Dialogue" beginning "The Holy Ghost shall come upon thee," &c. If ever one author quotes another, Justin in this place quotes St. Luke. They cannot be taken from the Protevangelium, because the corresponding words in the Protevangelium are very different from those in St. Luke; and the only real difference between Justin's quotation and St. Luke is that St. Luke reads, "shall be called the Son of God;" whereas Justin has "is the Son of God." Now in this Justin differs from the Protevangelium, which reads, "Shall be called the Son of the Highest;" so the probability is still more increased that in the quotation from the "Dialogue" he did not quote the Protevangelium, and did quote St. Luke. However, we will make the author a present of these words, because we want to assume for a moment the truth of his conclusion, which he thus expresses :—

" Justin's divergencies from the Protevangelium prevent our supposing that, in its present form, it could have been the actual source of his quotations ; but the wide differences which exist between the extant MSS. of the Protevangelium show that even the most ancient does not present it in its original form. It is much more probable that Justin had before him a still older work, to which both the Protevangelium and the third Gospel were indebted. (" Supernatural Religion," vol. i. p. 306.)

Assuming, then, the correctness of this, Justin had a still older Gospel than that of St. Luke; and we shall hereafter show that St. Luke's Gospel was used in all parts of the world in Justin's day, and long before it. Now Justin himself lived only 100 years after the Resurrection; and this is no very great age for the copy of a book, still less for the book itself, of which any one may convince himself by a glance around his library. We may depend upon it that Justin would have used the oldest sources of information. A book so old in Justin's days may have been published at the outset of Christianity. The author himself surmises that it may have been the work of one of St. Luke's πολλοί. Anyhow it is an older, and therefore, according to the writer's own line of argument all through his book, a more reliable witness to the things of Christ, and its witness is to the supernatural in His Birth. Are we, then, able to form any conjecture as to the name of this most ancient Gospel ? Yes. The author of " Supernatural Religion" identifies it with the lost Gospel to the Hebrews, in the words :—

" Much more probably, however, Justin quotes from the more ancient source from which the Protevangelium and perhaps St. Luke drew their narrative. There can be little doubt that the Gospel according to the Hebrews contained an account of the birth in Bethelehem, and as it is, at least, certain that Justin quotes other particulars from it, there is fair reason to believe that he likewise found this fact[1] in that work." (Vol. ii. p. 313.)

If, then, this be the Gospel from which Justin derived his account of the Nativity, it seems to have contained all the facts for which we have now to look into St. Matthew and St. Luke. It combined the testimonies of both Evangelists to the supernatural Birth of Jesus.

---

[1] That of our Lord being born in a cave.

Section V.

THE PRINCIPAL WITNESS.—HIS TESTIMONY
RESPECTING THE BAPTISM OF CHRIST.

THE next extract from Justin which I shall give is one describing our Lord's Baptism. This account, like almost every other given in the dialogue with Tripho, is mentioned by him, not so much for its own sake, but because it gave him opportunity to show the fulfilment, or supposed fulfilment, of a prophecy—in this case the prophecy of Isaiah that the " Spirit of the Lord should rest upon Him."

"Even at His birth He was in possession of His power; and as He grew up like all other men, by using the fitting means, He assigned its own [requirements] to each development, and was sustained by all kinds of nourishment, and waited for thirty years, more or less, until John appeared before Him as the herald of His approach, and preceded Him in the way of baptism, as I have already shown. And then, when Jesus had gone to the river Jordan, where John was baptizing, and when He had stepped into the water, a fire was kindled in the Jordan; and when He came out of the water, the Holy Ghost lighted on Him like a dove [as] the Apostles of this very Christ of ours wrote. . . . . . For when John remained (literally sat)[1] by the Jordan, and preached

---

[1] 'Ιωάννου γὰρ καθεζομένου.

the baptism of repentance, wearing only a leathern girdle and a vesture made of camel's hair, eating nothing but locusts and wild honey, men supposed him to be Christ; but he cried to them—'I am not the Christ, but the voice of one crying; for He that is stronger than I shall come, whose shoes I am not worthy to bear . . . .' The Holy Ghost, and for man's sake, as I formerly stated, lighted on Him in the form of a dove, and there came at the same instant from the heavens a voice, which was uttered also by David when he spoke, personating Christ, what the Father would say to Him, 'Thou art my Son, this day have I begotten Thee;' [the Father] saying that His generation would take place for men, at the time when they would become acquainted with Him. 'Thou art my Son; this day have I begotten Thee.'" (Ch. lxxxviii.)

The author of "Supernatural Religion" lays very great stress upon this passage, as indicating throughout sources of information different from our Gospels. He makes the most of the fact that John is said to have "sat" by the Jordan, not apparently remembering that sitting was the normal posture for preaching and teaching (Matthew v. 1; Luke iv. 20). He, of course, dwells much upon the circumstance that a fire was kindled in the Jordan at the time of our Lord's baptism, which additional instance of the supernatural Justin may have derived either from tradition or from the Gospel to the Hebrews. Above all, he dwells upon the fact—and a remarkable fact it is—that Justin supposes that the words of the Father were not "Thou art my beloved Son, in Thee I am well pleased," but "Thou art my Son, this day have I begotten Thee."

Now I do not for a moment desire to lessen the importance of the difficulty involved in a man, living in the age of Justin, giving the words of the Father so differently to what they appear in our Gospels. But what is the import of the discrepancy? It is simply a theological difficulty, the same in all respects with that which is involved in the application of these very words to the Resurrection of Christ by St. Paul, in Acts xiii. 33. It is in no sense a difficulty having the smallest bearing on the supernatural; for it is equally as supernatural for the Father to have said, with a voice audible to mortal ears, "This day have I begotten Thee," as it is for Him to have said, "In Thee I am well pleased."

What, then, is the inference which the author of "Supernatural Religion" draws from these discrepancies? This,—that Justin derived his information from the lost Gospel to the Hebrews.

"In the scanty fragments of the 'Gospel according to the Hebrews,' which have been preserved, we find both the incident of the fire kindled in Jordan, and the words of the heavenly voice, as quoted by Justin :—' And as He went out of the water, the heavens opened, and He saw the Holy Spirit of God in the form of a dove descend and enter into Him. And a voice was heard from heaven, saying, 'Thou art my beloved Son, in Thee I am well pleased;' and again, 'This day have I begotten Thee.' And immediately a great light shone in that place.' Epiphanius extracts this passage from the version in use among the Ebionites, but it is well known that there were many other varying forms of the same Gospel; and Hilgenfeld, with all probability, conjectures that the version known to Epiphanius was no longer in the same purity as that used by Justin, but represents the transition stage to the Canonical Gospels, adopting the words of the voice which they give without yet discarding the older form." ("Supernatural Religion," vol. i. p. 320.)

Here, then, are the remains of an older Gospel used by Justin, taken from copies which rationalists assert to have been, when used by him, in a state of greater purity than a subsequent recension; which subsequent recension was anterior to our present Gospels, and being older was purer, because nearer to the fountain-head of knowledge: but this older and purer form is characterized by a more pronounced supernatural element—to wit, the 'fire' in Jordan and the 'light'—so that, the older and purer the tradition, the more supernatural is its teaching.

THE PRINCIPAL WITNESS.—HIS TESTIMONY
RESPECTING THE DEATH OF CHRIST.

WE have now to consider the various notices in Justin respecting our Lord's Crucifixion, and the events immediately preceding and following it. Justin notices our Lord's entry into Jerusalem :—

"And the prophecy, 'binding His foal to the vine and washing His robe in the blood of the grape,' was a significant symbol of the things which were to happen to Christ, and of what He was to do. For the foal of an ass stood bound to a vine at the entrance of a village, and He ordered His acquaintances to bring it to Him then ; and when it was brought He mounted and sat upon it, and entered Jerusalem." (Apol. I. ch. xxxii.)

Justin in a subsequent place (Dial. ch. liii.) notices the fact only mentioned in St. Matthew, that Jesus commanded the disciples to bring both an ass and its foal :—

"And truly our Lord Jesus Christ, when He intended to go into Jerusalem, requested His disciples to bring Him a certain ass, along with its foal, which was bound in an entrance of a village called Bethphage ; and, having seated Himself on it, He entered into Jerusalem."

D

Justin thus describes the institution of the Eucharist :—

"For the Apostles, in the Memoirs composed by them, which are called Gospels, have thus delivered unto us what was enjoined upon them; that Jesus took bread, and, when He had given thanks, said, 'This do ye in remembrance of me, this is My body;' and that after the same manner, having taken the cup and given thanks, He said, 'This is My blood;' and gave it to them alone." (Apol. I. ch. lxvi.)

He thus adverts to the dispersion of the Apostles :—

"Moreover, the prophet Zechariah foretold that this same Christ would be smitten and His disciples scattered: which also took place. For after His Crucifixion the disciples that accompanied Him were dispersed." (Dial. ch. liii.)

He mentions our Lord's agony as the completion of a prophecy in Psalm xxii.:—

" For on the day on which He was to be crucified, having taken three of His disciples to the hill called Olivet, situated opposite to the temple at Jerusalem, He prayed in these words: 'Father, if it be possible, let this cup pass from Me.' And again He prayed, 'Not as I will, but as Thou wilt.'" (Dial. xcix.)

His sweating great drops of blood (mentioned only in St. Luke), also in fulfilment of Psalm xxii. :—

"For in the memoirs which I say were drawn up by His Apostles, and those who followed them [it is recorded] that His sweat fell down like drops of blood while He was pray-ing, and saying, 'If it be possible, let this cup pass.'"[1] (Ch. ciii.)

---

[1] Justin has ἱδρὼς ὡσεὶ θρόμβοι; St. Luke, ὁ ἱδρὼς αὐτοῦ ὡσεὶ θρόμβοι αἵματος. The author of "Supernatural Religion" lays great stress upon the omission of αἵματος, as indicating that Justin

His being sent to Herod (mentioned only in St. Luke) :—

" And when Herod succeeded Archelaus, having received the authority which had been allotted to him, Pilate sent to him by way of compliment Jesus bound; and God, fore-knowing that this would happen, had thus spoken, ' And they brought Him to the Assyrian a present to the king.' " (Ch. ciii.)

His silence before Pilate, also quoted by Justin, in fulfilment of Psalm xxii. :—

" And the statement, ' My strength is become dry like a potsherd, and my tongue has cleaved to my throat,' was also a prophecy of what would be done by Him according to the Father's will. For the power of His strong word, by which He always confuted the Pharisees and Scribes, and, in short, all your nation's teachers that questioned Him, had a cessation like a plentiful and strong spring, the waters of which have been turned off, when He kept silence, and chose to return no answer to any one in the presence of Pilate; as has been declared in the Memoirs of His Apostles." (Dial. ch. cii.)

His crucifixion :—

" And again, in other words, David in the twenty-first Psalm thus refers to the suffering and to the cross in a parable

---

did not know anything about St. Luke ; but we have to remember, first, that St. Luke alone mentions *any* sweat of our Lord in His agony ; secondly, that the account in Justin is said to be taken from " Memoirs drawn up by Apostles and *those who followed them*," *St. Luke being only one of those who followed;* thirdly, Justin and St. Luke both use a very scarce word, θρόμβοι ; fourthly, Justin and St. Luke both qualify this word by ὡσεὶ. If we add to this the fact that θρόμβοι seems naturally associated with blood in several authors, the probability seems almost to reach certainty, that Justin had St. Luke's account in his mind. The single omission is far more easy to be accounted for than the four coincidences.

of mystery: 'They pierced my hands and my feet; they counted all my bones; they considered and gazed upon me; they parted my garments among them, and cast lots upon my vesture.' For when they crucified Him, driving in the nails, they pierced His hands and feet; and those who crucified Him parted His garments among themselves, each casting lots for what he chose to have, and receiving according to the decision of the lot." (Ch. xcvii.)

The mocking of Him by His enemies:—

"And the following: 'All they that see Me laughed Me to scorn; they spake with the lips; they shook the head: He trusted in the Lord, let Him deliver Him since He desires Him;' this likewise He foretold should happen to Him. For they that saw Him crucified shook their heads each one of them, and distorted their lips, and, twisting their noses to each other, they spake in mockery the words which are recorded in the Memoirs of His Apostles, 'He said He was the Son of God: let Him come down; let God save Him.'" (Ch. ci.)

His saying, "My God, my God, why hast Thou forsaken Me?" (reported only in SS. Matthew and Mark):—

"For, when crucified, He spake, 'O God, my God, why hast Thou forsaken me?'" (Ch. xcix.)

His saying, "Father, into Thy hands I commend My Spirit," reported only in St. Luke:—

"For, when Christ was giving up His spirit on the cross, He said, 'Father, into Thy hands I commend my spirit,' as I have learned also from the Memoirs." (Ch. cv.)

His Resurrection and appearance to His Apostles gathered together (found only in SS. Luke and John), and His reminding the same Apostles that before His Death He had foretold it (found only in St. Luke):—

" And that He stood in the midst of His brethren, the Apostles (who repented of their flight from Him when He was crucified, after He rose from the dead, and after they were persuaded by Him that before His Passion He had mentioned to them that He must suffer these things, and that they were announced beforehand by the prophets)." [1] (Ch. cvi.)

The Jews spreading the report that His disciples had stolen away His Body by night (recorded only by St. Matthew):—

" Yet you not only have not repented, after you learned that He rose from the dead, but, as I said before, you have sent chosen and ordained men throughout all the world to proclaim that a godless and lawless heresy had sprung from one Jesus, a Galilean deceiver, whom we crucified, but His disciples stole Him by night from the tomb, where He was laid when unfastened from the cross." (Ch. cviii.)

The Apostles seeing the Ascension, and afterwards receiving power from Him in person, and going to every race of men:—

" And when they had seen Him ascending into heaven, and had believed, and had received power sent thence by Him upon them, and went to every race of men, they taught these things, and were called Apostles. " (Apol. i. ch. l.)

From all this the reader will see at a glance that Justin's view of the Crucifixion and the events attending it was exactly the same as ours. He will notice that all the events related in Justin are the same as those recorded in the Evangelists Matthew and Luke; and

---

1 And He said unto them, " These are the words which I spake unto you while I was yet with you, that all things must be fulfilled which were written in the law of Moses, and in the prophets, and in the Psalms concerning me." (Luke xxiii. 44.)

that the circumstances related by Justin, and not to be found in the Synoptics, are of the most trifling character, as, for instance, that the blaspheming by-standers at the cross " screwed up their noses." I think this is the only additional circumstance to which the writer of " Supernatural Religion " draws attention. He will notice that Justin records some events only to be found in St. Matthew and some only in St. Luke. He will notice also how frequently Justin reproduces the narrative rather than quotes it.

The ordinary reader would account for all this by sup-posing that Justin had our Synoptics (at least the first and third) before him, and reproduced incidents first from one and then from the other as they suited his purpose, and his purpose was not to give an account of the Crucifixion, but to elucidate the prophecies respecting the Crucifixion.

The author of " Supernatural Religion," however, goes through these citations, or supposed citations, seriatim, and attempts to show that each one must have been taken from some lost Gospel, most probably the Gospel of the Hebrews.

Be it so. Here, then, was a Gospel which contained all the separate incidents recorded in SS. Matthew and Luke, and, of course, combined them in one narrative. How is it that so inestimably valuable a Christian docu-ment was irretrievably lost, and its place supplied by three others, each far its inferior, each picking and choosing separate parts from the original; and that, about 120 years after the original promulgation of the Gospel, these three forged narratives superseded a Gospel which would have been, in the matter of our Lord's

Birth, Death, and Resurrection, a complete and perfect harmony ? I leave the author of " Supernatural Religion" to explain so unlikely a fact. One explanation is, however, on our author's own showing, inadmissible, which is, that our present Synoptics were adopted because they pandered more than the superseded one to the growing taste for the supernatural, for the earlier Gospel or Gospels contained supernatural incidents which are wanting in our present Synoptics.

THE PRINCIPAL WITNESS.—HIS TESTIMONY
RESPECTING THE MORAL TEACHING OF OUR LORD.

ONE more class of apparent quotations from our Synoptic Gospels must now be considered, viz., the citations in Justin of the moral teaching or precepts of Christ.   These are mostly to be found in one place, in one part of the First Apology (chapters xv.-xviii.), and they are introduced for the express purpose of convincing the Emperor of the high standard of Christ's moral teaching.

The author of " Supernatural Religion " gives very considerable extracts from these chapters, which I shall give in his own translation :—

" He (Jesus) spoke thus of chastity : ' Whosoever may have gazed on a woman, to lust after her, hath committed adultery already in the heart before God.' And, ' If thy right eye offend thee cut it out, for it is profitable for thee to enter into the kingdom of heaven with one eye (rather) than having two to be thrust into the everlasting fire.' And, ' Whosoever marrieth a woman, divorced from another man, committeth adultery.' "

*　　*　　*　　*　　*　　*　　*

"And regarding our affection for all He thus taught ' If ye love them which love you what new thing do ye ? for even the fornicators do this ; but I say unto you, pray for your enemies, and love them which hate you, and bless them which curse you, and offer prayer for them which despitefully use you.' And that we should communicate to the needy, and do nothing for praise, He said thus: ' Give ye to every one that asketh, and from him that desireth to borrow turn not ye away, for, if ye lend to them from whom ye hope to receive, what new thing do ye? for even the publicans do this. But ye, lay not up for yourselves upon the earth, where moth and rust doth corrupt, and robbers break through, but lay up for yourselves in the heavens, where neither moth nor rust doth corrupt. For what is a man profited if he shall gain the whole world but destroy his soul? or what shall he give in exchange for it? Lay up, therefore, in the heavens, where neither moth nor rust doth corrupt.' And, 'Be ye kind and merciful as your Father also is kind and merciful, and maketh His sun to rise on sinners, and just and evil. But be not careful what ye shall eat and what ye shall put on. Are ye not better than the birds and the beasts? and God feedeth them. Therefore be not careful what ye shall eat or what ye shall put on, for your heavenly Father knoweth that ye have need of these things; but seek ye the kingdom of the heavens, and all these things shall be added unto you, for where the treasure is there is also the mind of the man." And 'Do not these things to be seen of men, otherwise ye have no reward of your Father which is in heaven.' And regarding our being patient under injuries, and ready to help all, and free from anger, this is what He said: ' Unto him striking thy cheek offer the other also; and him who carrieth off thy cloak, or thy coat, do not thou prevent. But whosoever shall be angry is in danger of the fire. But every one who compelleth thee to go a mile, follow twain. And let your good works shine before men, so that, perceiving, they may adore your Father, which is in heaven.' . . . . And regarding our not swearing at all, but ever speaking the truth, He thus taught: ' Ye may not swear at all, but let your yea be yea, and your nay nay, for what is more than these is of the evil one.' "

* * * * * * *

" 'For not those who merely make profession, but those who do the work,' as He said, 'shall be saved.' For He spake thus : 'Not every one that saith unto me, Lord, Lord, shall (enter into the kingdom of heaven, but he that doeth the will of my Father, which is in heaven). For whosoever heareth me, and doeth what I say, heareth Him that sent me. But many will say to me, Lord, Lord, have we not eaten and drunk in Thy name, and done wonders ? And then will I say unto them, 'Depart from me, workers of iniquity.' There shall be weeping and gnashing of teeth, when indeed the righteous shall shine as the sun, but the wicked are sent into everlasting fire. For many shall arrive in My name, outwardly, indeed, clothed in sheep-skins, but inwardly being ravening wolves. Ye shall know them from their works, and every tree that bringeth not forth good fruit is hewn down and cast into the fire."

*　　　*　　　*　　　*　　　*

" As Christ declared, saying, ' To whom God has given more, of him shall more also be demanded again.' "

The ordinary reader, remembering that Justin was writing for the heathen, would suppose, after reading the above, that Justin reproduced from SS. Matthew and Luke the moral precepts of Christ, or rather those which suited his purpose, and his purpose was to show to the heathen Emperor that Christianity would make the best members of a community.

To this end he reproduces the precepts respecting chastity, respecting love to all, and communicating to the needy—being kind and merciful—not caring much for material things—being patient and truthful—and, above all, being sincere.

He did not reproduce the precepts respecting prayer, simply because immoral men among the heathen worshipped their gods as devoutly as moral men did. He did not reproduce the Lord's prayer, because he would not consider that it belonged to the heathen, or the promises that God would hear prayer, simply because these would belong to Christians only.

Again, he evidently altered and curtailed what the heathen would not understand, as for instance, in quoting our Lord's saying respecting "anger," he quoted it very shortly, because to have quoted at length the gradations of punishment for being "angry without a cause," for "calling a brother Raca" and "fool," would have been almost unintelligible to those unacquainted with Jewish customs.

The author of "Supernatural Religion" repudiates the idea that Justin, in any of these quotations, makes use of our present Gospels. He examines these [so-called] quotations seriatim at considerable length, for the purpose of showing that Justin's variations from our present Gospels imply another source of information. He considers (and in this I cannot agree with him, though I shall, for argument's sake, yield the point) that—

"The hypothesis that these quotations are from the canonical gospels requires the acceptance of the fact that Justin, with singular care, collected from distant and scattered portions of these gospels a series of passages in close sequence to each other ,forming a whole unknown to them, but complete in itself." ("Supernatural Religion," vol. i. p. 359.)

I say I cannot agree with this, because I think that the extracts I have given have all the signs of a piece of patchwork by no means well put together, but I will assume that he is right in his view.

Here, then, we have, according to his hypothesis, another sermon of Christ's, which, owing to the "close sequence" of its various passages, and its completeness as a whole, must take its place alongside of the Sermon on the Mount. Where does it come from ?—

"The simple and natural conclusion, supported by many strong reasons, is that Justin derived his quotations from a Gospel which was different from ours, though naturally by subject and design it must have been related to them." (Vol. i. p. 384.)

And in page 378 our author traces one of the passages of this " consecutive" discourse through an epistle ascribed to Clement of Rome to the " Gospel according to the Egyptians," which was in all probability a version of the " Gospel according to the Hebrews."

Here, then, is a Gospel, the Gospel to the Hebrews, which not only contained, as the author has shown, a harmony of the histories in SS. Matthew and Luke, so far, at least, as the Birth and Death of Christ are concerned, but also such a full and consecutive report of the moral teaching of Christ, that it may not unfitly be described as " a series of passages in close sequence to each other," collected " with singular care " " from distant and scattered portions of these Gospels." How, we ask, could such a Gospel have perished utterly ? A Gospel, which, besides containing records of the historical and supernatural much fuller than any one of the surviving Gospels, contained also a sort of Sermon on the Mount, amalgamating in one whole the moral teaching of our Lord, ought surely (if it ever was in existence) to have won its place in the canon.

THE PRINCIPAL WITNESS.—HIS TESTIMONY TO ST. JOHN.

WE have now to consider the citations (or supposed citations) of Justin from the fourth Gospel. These, as I have mentioned, are treated by the author of "Supernatural Religion" separately at the conclusion of his work.

Whatever internal coincidences there are between the contents of St. John and those of the Synoptics, the external differences are exceedingly striking, and it is not at all to my present purpose to keep this fact out of sight. The plan of St. John's Gospel is different, the style is different, the subjects of the discourses, the scene of action, the incidents, and (with one exception) the miracles, all are different.

Now this will greatly facilitate the investigation of the question as to whether any author had St. John before him when he wrote. There may be some uncertainty with respect to the quotations from the Synoptics, as to whether an early writer quotes one or other, or derives what he cites from some earlier source, as for instance from one of St. Luke's πολλοί.

But it cannot be so with St. John. A quotation of,

or reference to, any words of any discourse of our Lord, or an account of any transaction as reported by St. John, can be discerned in an instant. At least it can be at once seen that it cannot have been derived from the Synoptics, or from any supposed apocryphal or traditional sources from which the Synoptics derived their information.

The special object of this Gospel is the identification of the pre-existent nature of our Lord with the eternal Word, and following upon this, His relation to His Father on the one side, and to mankind on the other.

He is the only begotten of the Father, God being His own proper Father ($\H{\iota}\delta\iota o\varsigma$), and so He is equal to the Father in nature (John v. 18), and yet, as being a Son, He is subordinate, so that He represents Himself throughout as sent by the Father to do His will and speak His words.

With reference to mankind He is, before His Incarnation, the "Light that lighteth every man." After and through His Incarnation He is to man all in all. He is even in death the object of their Faith. He is the Mediator through whose very person God sends the Spirit. He is the Life, the Light, the Living Water, the Spiritual Food.

Justin Martyr repeatedly reproduces in various forms of expression the truth that Christ is the eternal "Word made flesh" and revealed as the "Only-begotten Son of God," thus :—

"The first power after God the Father and Lord of all is the Word, Who is also the Son, and of Him we will, in what follows, relate how He took flesh and became man." (Apol. I. ch. xxxii.)

Again :—

" I have already proved that He was the only-begotten of the Father of all things, being begotten in a peculiar manner (ἰδίως), Word and Power by Him, and having afterwards become man through the Virgin." (Dial. ch. cv.)

Now, we have in these two passages four or five characteristic expressions of St. John relating to our Lord, not to be found in any other Scripture writer. I say " in any other," for I believe that not only the Epistles of St. John, but also the Apocalypse, notwithstanding certain differences in style, are to be ascribed to St. John.

We have the term " Word " united with " the Son," and with " Only begotten," and said to be " properly (propriè, ἰδίως) begotten ; " a reminiscence of John v. 18, the only place in the New Testament where the adjective ἴδιος or its adverb ἰδίως is applied to the relations of the Father and the Son, and we have this Word becoming flesh and man.

Now Justin, in one of the places, writes to convince an heathen emperor; and, in the other, an unbelieving Jew; and so in each case he reproduces the sense of John i. 1 and 14, and not the exact words. It would have been an absurdity for him to have quoted St. John exactly, for, in such a case, he must have retained the words " we beheld his glory, the glory as," which would have simply detracted from the force of the passage, being unintelligible without some explanation.

Again, we have in the Dialogue (ch. lxi.) the words "The Word of Wisdom, Who is Himself this God begotten of the Father of all things." Now here there seems to be a reproduction of the old and very probably original reading of John i. 18,[1] " The only begotten God who is in the bosom of the Father." Certainly this reading of John i. 18 is the only place where the idea of being begotten is associated with the term " God."

We next have to notice that Justin repeatedly uses the words " God " and " Lord " in collocation as applied to Jesus Christ; not " the Lord God," the usual Old Testament collocation, but God and Lord, thus :

" For Christ is King and Priest and God and Lord," &c. (Dial. ch. xxxiv.)

Again :—

" There is, and there is said to be, another God and Lord subject to the Maker of all things." (Dial. lvi.)

Now the only Gospel in which these words are to be found together and applied to Christ is that according to St. John, where he records the confession of St. Thomas, " My Lord and my God " (John xx. 28).

Again : St. John alone of the Evangelists speaks of our Lord as He that cometh from above (ὁ ἄνωθεν ἐρχό-μενος), as coming from heaven, as " leaving the world and going to the Father " (John iii. 31; xvi. 28), and Justin reproduces this in the words :—

" It is declared [by David in Prophecy,] that He would come forth from the highest heavens, and again return to the same places, in order that you may recognize Him as God coming forth from above and man living among men." (Dial. ch. lxiv.)

---

[1] It is the reading of Codices B and C of the Codex Sinaiticus of the Syriac, and of a number of Fathers and Versions.

Again: though St. John asserts by implication the equality in point of nature of the Father and the Son (John v. 18), yet he also very repeatedly records words of Christ which assert His subordination to the Father. Nowhere in the Synoptics do we read such words as " I can of mine own self do nothing :" " I seek not mine own will, but the will of the Father which hath sent me " (John v. 30) : " My meat is to do the will of Him that sent me, and to finish His work" (iv. 34; also John vi. 38) : " I have not spoken of myself; but the Father which sent me, He gave me a commandment, what I should say, and what I should speak." (xii. 49.)

Now Justin Martyr reproduces these intimations of the subordination of the Son :—

" Who is also called an Angel, because He announces to men whatsoever the Maker of all things, above Whom there is no other God, wishes to announce to them." (Dial. ch. lvi.)

Again :—

" I affirm that He has never at any time done anything which He Who made the world, above Whom there is no other God, has not wished Him both to do and to engage Himself with." (Dial. lvi.)

Again :—

" Boasts not in accomplishing anything through His own will or might." (Ch. ci.)

Let the reader clearly understand that I do not lay any stress whatsoever on these passages taken by themselves or together; but taken in connection with the intimation of the Word and Sonship asserted in St. John, and reproduced by Justin, they are very significant indeed.

E

St. John asserts that Jesus is the Word and the Only Begotten—that He is " Lord " and " God," and equal with the Father as being His Son (v. 18); but, lest men conceive of the Word as an independent God, he asserts the subordination of the Son as consisting, not in inferiority of nature, but in submission of will.

Justin reproduces in the same terms the teaching of St. John respecting the Logos—that the Logos was the Only Begotten, God-begotten, Lord and God. And then, lest his adversaries should assume from this that Christ was an independent God, he guards it by the assertion of the same doctrine of subordination of will; neither the doctrine nor the safeguard being expressly stated in the Synoptics, but contained in them by that wondrous implication by which one part of Divine truth really presupposes and involves all truth.

We have now to consider St. John's teaching respecting the relation of the Logos to man. One aspect of this doctrine is peculiar to St. John, and is as mysterious and striking a truth as we have in the whole range of Christian dogma.

It is contained in certain words in the exordium of the Fourth Gospel : " That [Word] was the true light which lighteth every man that cometh into the world."

This passage embodies a truth which is unique in Scripture : that in the Word was Life, that the Life was the Light of men, and that that Light was (even before the Incarnation) the true Light which lighteth every man.

This, I say, is a truth which is not, that I am aware of, to be found, except by very remote implication, in the rest of Scripture. And yet it is continually reproduced by Justin in a way which shows that he had drunk it in, as it were, and he used it continually as the principle on which to explain the vestiges of truth which existed among the heathen. Thus:—

" We have been taught that Christ is the first-born of God, and we have declared above that He is the Word of Whom every race of men were partakers; and those who lived reasonably (or with the Logos, οἱ μετὰ λόγου βιώσαντες) are Christians, even though they have been thought Atheists ; as among the Greeks, Socrates and Heraclitus, and men like them." (Apol. I. ch. xlvi.)

Again :—

" No one trusted in Socrates so as to die for this doctrine, but in Christ, Who was partially known even by Socrates (for He was and is the Word Who is in every man)," &c. (Apol. II. ch. x.)

Again, in a noble passage :—

" For each man spoke well in proportion to the share he had of the spermatic Divine Word,[1] seeing what was related to it. But they who contradict themselves in the more important points appear not to have possessed the heavenly wisdom, and the knowledge which cannot be spoken against. Whatever things were rightly said among all men are the property of us Christians." (Apol. II. xiii.)

There cannot, then, be the smallest doubt but that Justin's mind was permeated by a doctrine of the Logos exactly such as he would have derived from the diligent study of the fourth Gospel. But may he not have derived all this from Philo? No; because, if so, he would have referred Trypho, a Jew, to Philo, his brother Jew,

---

[1] "Εκαστος γάρ τις ἀπὸ μέρους τοῦ σπερματικοῦ θείου λόγου τὸ συγγενὲς ὁρῶν καλῶς ἐφθέγξατο.

which he never does. The speciality of St. John's teaching is not that he, like Plato or Philo, elaborates a Logos doctrine, but that once for all, with the authority of God, he identifies the Logos with the Divine Nature of our Lord. No other Evangelist or sacred writer does this, and he does.

THE PRINCIPAL WITNESS.—HIS FURTHER TESTIMONY
TO ST. JOHN.

WE now come to Justin's account of Christian
Baptism, which runs thus:—

"I will also relate the manner in which we dedicated
ourselves to God when we had been made new through
Christ, lest, if we omit this, we seem to be unfair in the
explanation we are making. As many as are persuaded
and believe that what we teach and say is true, and undertake to be able to live accordingly, are instructed to pray
and to entreat God with fasting, for the remission of their
sins that are past, we praying and fasting with them. Then
they are brought by us where there is water, and are
regenerated in the same manner in which we were ourselves
regenerated. For in the name of God, the Father and
Lord of the Universe, and of our Saviour Jesus Christ, and
of the Holy Spirit, they then receive the washing with
water. For Christ also said, 'Except ye be born again,
ye shall not enter into the Kingdom of Heaven.' Now, that
it is impossible for those who have once been born to enter
into their mothers' wombs, is manifest to all." (Apol. i.
ch. lxi.)

Now, taking into consideration the fact that St. John
is the only writer who sets forth our Lord as connecting
a birth with water [except a man be born of water and of
the Spirit]; that when our Lord does this it is (according

to St. John, and St. John only) following upon the
assertion that he must be born again, and that St. John
alone puts into the mouth of the objector the impossibility of a natural birth taking place twice, which Justin
notices; taking these things into account, it does seem
to me the most monstrous hardihood to deny that Justin
was reproducing St. John's account.

To urge trifling differences is absurd, for Justin, if he
desired to make himself understood, could not have
quoted the passage verbatim, or anything like it. For,
if he had, he must have prefaced it with some account of
the interview with Nicodemus, and he would have to
have referred to another Gospel to show that our Lord
alluded to baptism; for, though our Lord mentions
water, He does not here categorically mention baptism.
So, consequently, Justin would have to have said, " If
you refer to one of our Memoirs you will find certain
words which lay down the necessity of being born again,
and seem to connect this birth in some way with water,
and if you look into another Memoir you will see how
this can be, for you will find a direction to baptize with
water in the name of the Godhead, and if you put these
two passages together you will be able to understand
something of the nature of our dedication, and of the
way in which it is to be performed, and of the blessing
which we have reason to expect in it if we repent of
our sins."

Well, instead of such an absurd and indirect way of proceeding, which presupposes that Antoninus Pius was well
acquainted with the Diatessaron, he simply reproduces
the substance of the doctrine of St. John, and inter-
weaves with it the words of institution as found in

St. Matthew. I shall afterwards advert to the hypothesis that this account was taken from an apocryphal
Gospel.

Again, St. John is the only Evangelist who, in apparent allusion to the devout and spiritual reception of the
Inward Part of the Lord's Supper, speaks of it as eating
the Flesh of Christ, and drinking His Blood; the
Synoptics and St. Paul in 1 Cor. x. 11, always speaking of it as His *Body* and Blood. Now Justin, in describing the Sacrament of the Lord's Supper, uses the
language peculiar to St. John as well as that of the
Synoptics:—

" So likewise have we been taught that the food which
is blessed by the prayer of His word, and from which
our blood and flesh by transmutation are nourished, is the
flesh and blood of that Jesus Who was made flesh. For the
Apostles, in the Memoirs composed by them, which are called
Gospels, have thus delivered unto us what was enjoined upon
them ; that Jesus took bread, and when He had given thanks,
said, ' This do ye in remembrance of me. This is my body,' "
&c. (Apol. I. ch. lxvi.)

This, of course, would be a small matter itself, but,
taken in connection with the adoption of St. John's
language in regard of the other sacrament a very short
time before, it is exceedingly significant.

Again, St. John is the only Evangelist who records
our Lord's reference to the brazen serpent as typical of
Himself lifted up upon the Cross. Justin cites the same
incident as typical of Christ's Death, and, moreover,
cites our Lord's language as it is recorded in St. John,
respecting His being lifted up that men might believe
in Him and be saved:—

" For by this, as I previously remarked, He proclaimed the mystery, by which He declared that He would break the power of the serpent which occasioned the transgression of Adam, and [would bring] to them that believe on Him by this sign, i. e., Him Who was to be crucified, salvation from the fangs of the serpent, which are wicked deeds, idolatries, and other unrighteous acts. Unless the matter be so understood, give me a reason why Moses set up the brazen serpent for a sign, and bade those that were bitten gaze at it, and the wounded were healed." (Dial. ch. xciv.)

Again, St. John is the only Evangelist who records that the Baptist " confessed, and denied not, but confessed, ' I am not the Christ.' " Justin cites these very words as said by the Baptist :—

" For when John remained (or sat) by the Jordan . . . . men supposed him to be Christ, but he cried to them, ' I am not the Christ, but the voice of one crying,' " &c. (Dial. ch. lxxxviii.)

Again, St. John is the only Evangelist who puts into the mouth of our Blessed Lord, when He was accused of breaking the Sabbath, the retort that the Jews on the Sabbath Day circumcise a man . . . . that the law of Moses should not be broken. (John vii. 22.) And Justin also reproduces this in his Dialogue :—

" For, tell me, did God wish the priests to sin when they offer the sacrifices on the Sabbaths ? or those to sin who are circumcised, or do circumcise, on the Sabbaths ; since He commands that on the eighth day—even though it happen to be a Sabbath—those who are born shall be always circumcised ?" (Dial. ch. xxvii.)

Again, St. John represents our Lord, when similarly harassed by the Jews, as appealing to the upholding of all things by God on the Sabbath as well as on any other

day, in the words, " My Father worketh hitherto, and I
work." (John v. 17.) And Justin very shortly after
uses the same argument :—

" Think it not strange that we drink hot water on the
Sabbath, since God directs the government of the universe on
this day, equally as on all others; and the priests on other
days, so on this, are ordered to offer sacrifices." (Dial. ch.
xxix.)

It is very singular that Justin, whilst knowing nothing
of St. John, should, on a subject like this, use two arguments peculiar to St. John, and not to be found in
disputes on the very same subject in the Synoptics.

Again, St. John alone records that Jesus healed a
man " blind from his birth," and notices that the Jews
themselves were impressed with the greatness of the
miracle. (John ix. 16, 32.) Justin remarks, " In that
we say that He made whole the lame, the paralytic, and
those born blind." (Apol. i. ch. xxii.)

Again, St. John is the only Evangelist who makes
our Lord to say, " Now I tell you before it come, that
when it is come to pass ye may believe." (John xiii.
19; xiv. 29; xvi. 4.) And Justin adopts and amplifies
this very sentiment with reference to the use of prophecy :—

" For things which were incredible, and seemed impossible
with men, these God predicted by the Spirit of prophecy as
about to come to pass, in order that, when they came to pass,
there might be no unbelief, but faith, because of their prediction." (Apol. i. ch. xxxiii.)

Again, St. John alone of the Evangelists records that
our Lord used with the unbelieving Jews the argument

that they believed not Moses, for, had they believed Moses, they would have believed Him, for Moses wrote of Him. (John, v. 46, 47.) And Justin reproduces in substance the same argument:—

"For though ye have the means of understanding that this man is Christ from the signs given by Moses, yet you will not." (Dial. xciii.)

Again, St. John is the only sacred writer who speaks of our Lord "giving the living water," and causing that water to flow from men's hearts, and Justin (somewhat inaccurately) reproduces the figure:—

"And our hearts are thus circumcised from evil, so that we are happy to die for the name of the Good Rock, which causes living water to burst forth for the hearts of those who by Him have loved the Father of all, and which gives those who are willing to drink of the water of life." (Dial. ch. cxiv.)

Again, St. John alone records that Christ spake of Himself as the Light, and Justin speaks of Him as "the only blameless and righteous Light sent by God." (Dial. ch. xvii.)

Again, St. John alone speaks of our Lord as representing Himself to be the true vine, and His people as the branches. Justin uses the same figure with respect to the people or Church of God:—

"Just as if one should cut away the fruit-bearing parts of a vine, it grows up again, and yields other branches flourishing and fruitful; even so the same thing happens to us. For the vine planted by God and Christ the Saviour is His People." (Dial. ch. cx.)

Again, St. John alone represents our Saviour as saying, "I have power to lay [my life] down, and

I have power to take it again. This commandment have I received of my Father." (John x. 18.) And Justin says of Christ that, in fulfilment of a certain prophecy,—

" He is to do something worthy of praise and wonderment, being about to rise again from the dead on the third day after the Crucifixion, and this He has obtained from the Father." (Dial. ch. c.)

Some of these last instances which I have given are reminiscences rather than reproductions; but like all other reminiscences they imply things remembered, sometimes not perfectly correctly, and so not applied as applied in the original; but they are all real reminiscences of words and things to be found only in our fourth Gospel.

THE PRINCIPAL WITNESS.—HIS TESTIMONY
SUMMED UP.

FROM all this it is clear that Justin had not only seen and reverenced St. John's Gospel, but that his mind was permeated with its peculiar teaching.

I hesitate not to say that, if a man rejects the evidence above adduced, he rejects it because on other grounds he is determined, cost what it may, to discredit the Fourth Gospel.

Let us briefly recapitulate.

Justin reproduced the doctrine of the Logos, using the words of St. John. He asserted the Divine and human natures of the Son of God in the words of St. John, or in exactly similar words. He reproduced that peculiar teaching of our Lord, to be found only in St. John, whereby we are enabled to hold the true and essential Godhead of Christ without for a moment holding that He is an independent God. He reproduced the doctrine of the Logos being, even before His Incarnation, in *every* man as the " true light " to enlighten him.

He reproduces the doctrine of the Sacraments in terms to be found only in the Fourth Gospel. He reproduces, or alludes to, arguments and types and prophecies and historical events, only to be found in St. John's Gospel.

It seems certain, then, that if Justin was acquainted with any one of our four Gospels, that Gospel was the one according to St. John.

What answer, the reader will ask, does the author of "Supernatural Religion" give to all this? Why, he simply ignores the greater part of these references (we trust through ignorance of their existence), and takes notice of some three or four, in which, to use the vulgar expression, he picks holes, by drawing attention to discrepancies of language or application, and dogmatically pronounces that Justin could not have known the fourth Gospel.

Well, then, the reader will ask, from whom did Justin derive the knowledge of doctrines and facts so closely resembling those contained in St. John?

Again, we have reference to supposed older sources of information which have perished. With respect to the Logos doctrine, the author of "Supernatural Religion" asserts :—

"His [Justin's] doctrine of the Logos is precisely that of Philo, and of writings long antecedent to the fourth Gospel, and there can be no doubt, we think, that it was derived from them." ("Supernatural Religion," vol. ii. p. 297.)

It may be well here to remark that, strictly speaking, there is no Logos *doctrine* in St. John's Gospel,—by doctrine meaning "scientifically expressed doctrine," drawn out, and expounded at length, as in Philo. The Gospel commences with the assertion that the Logos, Whoever He be, is God, and is the pre-existent Divine nature of

Jesus; he does this once and once only, and never recurs to it afterwards.

The next passage referred to is the assertion of the Baptist, "I am not the Christ," and the conclusion of the author is that " there is every reason to believe that he derived it from a particular Gospel, in all probability the Gospel according to the Hebrews, different from ours." (Vol. ii. p. 302.)

The last place noticed is Justin's reproduction of John iii. 3-5, in connection with the institution of baptism. After discussing this at some length, for the purpose of magnifying the differences and minimizing the resemblances, his conclusion is :—

" As both the Clementines and Justin made use of the Gospel according to the Hebrews, the most competent critics have, with reason, adopted the conclusion that the passage we are discussing was derived from that Gospel ; at any rate it cannot for a moment be maintained as a quotation from our fourth Gospel, and it is of no value as evidence for its existence." ("Supernatural Religion," vol. ii. p. 313.)

We have now tolerably full means of judging what a wonderful Gospel this Gospel to the Hebrews must have been, and what a loss the Church has sustained by its extinction.

Here was a Gospel which contained a harmony of the history, moral teaching, and doctrine of all the four. As we have seen, it contained an account of the miraculous Birth and Infancy, embodying in one narrative the facts contained in the first and third Gospels. It contained a narrative of the events preceding and attending our Lord's Death, far fuller and more complete than that of any single Gospel in the Canon. It contained a record of the teaching of Christ, similar to our present Sermon on the Mount, embodying the teaching scattered up and down in all parts of SS. Matthew and Luke, and in addition to all this it embodied the very peculiar tradition, both in respect of doctrine and of history, of the fourth Gospel.

How could it possibly have happened that a record of the highest value, on account both of its fulness and extreme antiquity, should have perished, and have been superseded by four later and utterly unauthentic productions, one its junior by at least 120 years, and each one of these deriving from it only a part of its teaching ; the first three, for no conceivable reason, rejecting all that peculiar doctrine now called Johannean, and the fourth confining itself to reproducing this so-called Johannean element and this alone ? It is only necessary to state this to show the utter absurdity of the author's hypothesis.

But the marvel is that a person assuming such airs of penetration and research[1] should not have perceived that,

---

[1] For instance, in vol. ii. p. 42, &c., he speaks of one of Tischendorf's assertions as " a conclusion the audacity of which can scarcely be exceeded."—Then, " This is, however, almost surpassed by the treatment of Canon Westcott."—Then, " The unwarranted inference of Tischendorf."—" There is no ground for Tischendorf's assumption." —" Tischendorf, the self-constituted modern Defensor Fidei, asserts with an assurance which can scarcely be characterized otherwise than as an unpardonable calculation upon the ignorance of his readers."—" Canon Westcott says, with an assurance which, considering the nature of the evidence, is singular."—" Even Dr. Westcott states," &c.—For Tertullian his contempt seems unbounded : indeed we may say the same of all the Fathers. Numberless times does he speak of their " uncritical spirit." The only person for whom he seems to have a respect is the heretic Marcion. Even rationalists, such as Credner and Ewald, are handled severely when they differ from him. The above are culled from a few pages.

if he has proved his point, he has simply strengthened the evidence for the supernatural, for he has proved the existence of a fifth Gospel, far older and fuller than any we now possess, witnessing to the supernatural Birth, Life, Death, and Resurrection of Jesus.

The author strives to undermine the evidence for the authenticity of our present Gospels for an avowedly dogmatic purpose. He believes in the dogma of the impossibility of the supernatural; he must, for this purpose, discredit the witness of the four, and he would fain do this by conjuring up the ghost of a defunct Gospel, a Gospel which turns out to be far more emphatic in its testimony to the supernatural and the dogmatic than any of the four existing ones, and so the author of this pretentious book seems to have answered himself. His own witnesses prove that from the first there has been but one account of Jesus of Nazareth.

THE PRINCIPAL WITNESS ON OUR LORD'S GODHEAD.

THE author of "Supernatural Religion" has directed his attacks more particularly against the authenticity of the Gospel according to St. John. His desire to discredit this Gospel seems at times to arise out of a deep personal dislike to the character of the disciple whom Jesus loved. (Vol. ii. pp. 403-407, 427, 428, &c.)

On the author's principles, it is difficult to understand the reason for such an attack on this particular Gospel. He is not an Arian or Socinian (as the terms are commouly understood), who might desire to disparage the testimony of this Gospel to the Pre-existence and Godhead of our Lord. His attack is on the Supernatural generally, as witnessed to by any one of the four Gospels; and it is allowed on all hands that the three Synoptics were written long before the Johannean; and, besides this, he has proved to his own satisfaction, and to the satisfaction of the Reviewers who so loudly applauded his work, that there existed a Gospel long anterior to the Synoptics, which is more explicit in its declarations of the Supernatural than all of them put together.

F

However, as he has made a lengthened and vigorous attempt to discredit this Gospel especially, it may be well to show his extraordinary misconceptions respecting the mere contents of the Fourth Gospel, and the opinions of the Fathers (notably Justin Martyr) who seem to quote from it, or to derive their doctrine from it.

The first question—and by far the most important one which we shall have to meet—is this: Is the doctrine respecting the Person of Jesus more fully developed in the pages of Justin Martyr, or in the Fourth Gospel? We mean by the doctrine respecting the Person of Jesus, that He is, with reference to His pre-existent state, the Logos and Only-begotten Son of God; and that, as being such, He is to be worshipped and honoured as Lord and God; and that, in order to be our Mediator, and the Sacrifice for our sin, He took upon Him our nature.

The author of " Supernatural Religion " endeavours to trace the doctrine of the Logos, as contained in Justin, to older sources than our present Fourth Gospel, particularly to Philo and the Gospel according to the Hebrews. The latter is much too impalpable to enable us to verify his statements by it; but we shall have to show his misconceptions respecting the connection of Justin's doctrine with the former. What we have now to consider is the following statement:—

" It is certain, however, that both Justin and Philo, unlike the prelude to the Fourth Gospel (i. 1), place the Logos in a secondary position to God the Father, another point indicating a less advanced stage of the doctrine."

From this we must, of course, infer that the author of " Supernatural Religion " considers that Justin does not state the essential Godhead of the Second Person as distinctly and categorically as it is stated in the Fourth Gospel. And as it is assumed by Rationalists that there was in the early Church a constantly increasing development of the doctrine of the true Godhead of our Lord, gradually superseding some earlier doctrine of an Arian, or Humanitarian, or Sadducean type; therefore, the more fully developed doctrine of the Godhead of our Lord in any book proves that book to be of later origin than another book in which it is not so fully developed.

The author of " Supernatural Religion" cannot deny that Justin ascribes the names "Lord" and "God" and Pre-existence before all worlds to Jesus as the Logos, but he fastens upon certain statements or inferences respecting the subordination of the Son to the Father, and His acting for His Father, or under Him, in the works of Creation and Redemption, which Justin, as an orthodox believer who would abhor Tritheism, was bound to make, and most ignorantly asserts that such statements are contrary to the spirit of the Fourth Gospel.

I shall now set before the reader the statements of both St. John and Justin respecting the Divine Nature of our Lord, so that he may judge for himself which is the germ and which the development.

The Fourth Gospel once, and once only, sets forth the Godhead and Pre-existence of the Logos, and this is in the exordium or prelude :—

" In the beginning was the Word, and the Word was with God, and the Word was God."

The Fourth Gospel once, and once only, identifies this

Word with the pre-existent nature of Jesus, in the concluding words of the same exordium :—

"The Word was made flesh and dwelt among us, and we beheld His Glory, the glory as of the Only-begotten of the Father, full of grace and truth."

Except in these two places (and, of course, I need not say that they are all-important as containing by implication the whole truth of God respecting Christ), there is no mention whatsoever of the "Word" in this Gospel.

The Fourth Gospel gives to Jesus the name of God only in two places, *i. e.* in the narrative of the second appearance of our Lord to His apostles assembled together after His Resurrection, where Thomas is related to have said to Him the words, "My Lord and my God ;" and in the words "The Word was God" taken in connection with "the Word was made flesh." The indirect, but certain, proofs by implication that Jesus fully shared with His Father the Divine Nature are numerous, as, for instance, that He wields all the power of Godhead, in that "whatsoever things [the Father] doeth these doeth the Son likewise"—that He is equal in point of nature with the Father, because God is His own proper Father (ἴδιος)—that He raises from the dead whom He wills—that He and the Father are One—that when Esaias saw the glory of God in the temple he saw Christ's glory; and, because of all this, He is the object of faith, even of the faith which saves.

But, as my purpose is not to show that either Justin or St. John hold the Godhead of our Lord, but rather to compare the statements of the one with the other; and, inasmuch as to cite the passages in which Justin Martyr assumes that our Blessed Lord possesses all Divine attributes would far exceed the limits which I have proposed to myself, I shall not further cite the passages in St. John, which only *imply* our Lord's Godhead, but proceed to cite the *direct* statements of Justin (or rather some of them) on this head.

Whereas, then, St. John categorically asserts the Godhead of our Lord in one, or, at the most, two places, Justin directly asserts it nearly forty times.

The following are noticeable :—

" And Trypho said, You endeavour to prove an incredible and well-nigh impossible thing; [namely] that God endured to be born and become man.[1] If I undertook, said I, [Justin] to prove this by doctrines or arguments of men, you should not bear with me. But if I quote frequently Scriptures, and so many of them, referring to this point, and ask you to comprehend them, you are hard-hearted in the recognition of the mind and will of God." (Dial. ch. lxviii.)

Again :—

" This very Man Who was crucified is proved to have been set forth expressly as God and Man, and as being crucified and as dying."[2] (Dial. ch. lxxi.)

Again, Justin accuses the Jews of having mutilated the Prophetical Scriptures, by having cut out of them the following prophecy respecting our Lord's descent into hell :—

" The Lord God remembered His dead people of Israel who lay in the graves; and He descended to preach to them His own Salvation." (Dial. ch. lxxii.)

---

[1] Ὅτι Θεὸς ὑπέμεινε γεννηθῆναι καὶ ἄνθρωπος γενέσθαι.

[2] Ἐξ ὧν διαῤῥήδην οὗτος αὐτὸς ὁ σταυρωθεὶς ὅτι Θεὸς καὶ ἄνθρωπος, καὶ σταυρούμενος καὶ ἀποθνήσκων κεκηρυγμένος ἀποδείκνυται.

Again :—

" For Christ is King, and Priest, and God, and Lord, and Angel, and Man, and Captain, and Stone, and a Son born, and first made subject to suffering, then returning to heaven, and again coming with glory." (Dial. xxxiv.)

Again :—

" Now you will permit me first to recount the prophecies, which I wish to do in order to prove that Christ is called both God, and Lord of Hosts, and Jacob in parable, by the Holy Spirit." (Dial. ch. xxxvi.)

Again, Justin makes Trypho to say :—

" When you [Justin] say that this Christ existed as God before the ages, then that He submitted to be born, and become man, yet that He is not man of man, this [assertion] appears to me to be not merely paradoxical, but also foolish. And I replied to this, I know that the statement does appear to be paradoxical, especially to those of your race, who are ever unwilling to understand or to perform the [requirements] of God." (Dial. ch. xlviii.)

Again, Justin makes Trypho demand :—

" Answer me then, first, how you can show that there is another God besides the Maker of all things ; [1] and then you will show [further], that He submitted to be born of the Virgin.

" I replied, Give me permission first of all to quote certain passages from the Prophecy of Isaiah which refer to the office of forerunner discharged by John the Baptist." (Dial. l.)

---

[1] The reader must remember that Justin puts this expression, which seems to imply a duality of Godhead, into the mouth of an adversary. In other places, as I shall show, he very distinctly guards against such a notion, by asserting the true and proper Sonship of the Word and His perfect subordination to His Father. There is a passage precisely similar in ch. lv.

Lastly —:

" Now, assuredly, Trypho, I shall show that, in the vision of Moses, this same One alone, Who is called an Angel, and Who is God, appeared to and communed with Moses . . . . . Even so here, the Scriptures, in announcing that the angel of the Lord appeared unto Moses, and in afterwards declaring Him to be Lord and God, speaks of the same One, Whom it declares by the many testimonies already quoted to be minister to God, Who is above the world, above Whom there is no other." (Dial. ch. lx.)

In order not to weary the reader, I give the remainder in a note.[1]

---

[1] "I continued: Moreover, I consider it necessary to repeat to you the words which narrate how He is both Angel and God and Lord, and Who appeared as a Man to Abraham." (Dial. ch. lviii.)

" Permit me, further, to show you from the Book of Exodus, how this same One, Who is both Angel, and God, and Lord, and Man." (Dial. ch. lix.)

"God begat before all creatures, a Beginning, a certain rational Power from Himself, Who is called by the Holy Spirit, now the Glory of the Lord, now the Son, again Wisdom, again an Angel, then God, and then Lord and Logos." (Dial. ch. lxi.)

" The Word of Wisdom, Who is Himself this God, begotten of the Father of all things, and Word, and Wisdom, and Power, and the Glory of the Begetter, will bear evidence to me," &c. (Dial. lxi.)

" Therefore these words testify explicitly that He is witnessed to by Him Who established these things [*i.e.* the Father] as deserving to be worshipped, as God and as Christ." (Dial. lxiii.)

The reader will find other declarations, most of which are equally explicit, in Dial. ch. lvi. (at the end), ch. lvii. (at the end), lxii. (middle), lxviii. (at middle and end), lxxiv. (middle), lxxv., lxxvi. (made Him known, being Christ, as God strong and to be worshipped), lxxxv. (twice called the Lord of Hosts), lxxxvii. (where Christ is declared to be pre-existent God), cxiii. (he [Joshua] was neither Christ, Who is God, nor the Son of God), cxv. (our Priest, Who is God, and Christ, the Son of God, the Father of all), cxxiv. (Now I have proved at length that Christ is called God), cxxv. (He ministered to the will of the Father, yet nevertheless is God), cxxvi. (thrice in this chapter), cxxvii., cxxviii., cxxix.

The reader will observe that the assertions of Justin, which I have given, are the strongest that could be made by any one who holds the Godhead of Christ, and yet holds that that Godhead is not an independent Divine Existence, but derived from the Father Who begat Him, and, by begetting, fully communicated to His Son or Offspring His own Godhead.

From these extracts the reader will be able to judge for himself whether the doctrine of St. John is the expansion or development of that of Justin, or the doctrine of Justin the development of that of St. John.

He will also be able to judge of the absurdity of supposing that after the time of Justin the cause of Orthodoxy demanded the forgery of a Gospel, in order to set forth more fully the Divine Glory of the Redeemer.

THE PRINCIPAL WITNESS ON THE DOCTRINE OF
THE LOGOS.

WE have now to compare Justin's doctrine of the Logos with that of the Fourth Gospel.

The doctrine or dogma of the Logos is declared in the Fourth Gospel in a short paragraph of fourteen verses, a part of which is occupied with the mission of the Baptist.

The doctrine, as I have said before, is rather oracular enunciation than doctrine; *i. e.* it is not doctrine elaborately drawn out and explained and guarded, but simply laid down as by the authority of Almighty God.

It is contained in four or five direct statements :—

" In the beginning was the Logos."

In the beginning—that is, before all created things— when there was no finite existence by which time could be measured ; in that fathomless abyss of duration when there was God only :—

" The Logos was with God."

Though numerically distinct from Him,[1] He was so " by " or " with " Him as to be His fellow:—

---

[1] I adopt this phrase because it is used by Justin. His words are ἀριθμῷ ὄντα ἕτερον. (Dial. ch. lxii.)

" The Logos was God."

That is, though numerically distinct, He partook of the same Divine Nature:

" All Things were made by Him."

Because, partaking fully of the nature, He partook fully of the power of God, and so of His creating power.

" That was the true light which lighteth every man that cometh into the world."

" The Logos was made flesh."

He was incarnate by the Holy Ghost of the Virgin Mary, and was made man.

The first enunciation, then, of St. John is that—

" IN THE BEGINNING WAS THE WORD."

In Justin we read :—

" His Son, Who alone is properly called Son, the Word, Who also was with Him, and was begotten before the works." Apol. II. ch. vi.)

Again :—

" When you [Justin] say that this Christ existed as God before the ages."   (Dial. ch. xlviii.)

Again:—

" God begat before all creatures a Beginning,[1] [who was] a certain rational Power from Himself, Who is called by the Holy Spirit, now the Glory of the Lord, now the Son, again Wisdom, again an Angel, then God, and then Lord and Logos."   (Dial. ch. lxi.)

Now it is to be here remarked, that though the Logos is continually declared to be " begotten of," " derived

---

[1] Ὅτι ἀρχὴν πρὸ πάντων τῶν κτισμάτων ὁ Θεὸς γεγέννηκε δύναμίν τινα ἐξ ἑαυτοῦ λογικήν, κ.τ.λ.

from," " an offspring of " the Father, yet in no case is
He declared to be "created" or "made," anticipating
the declaration which we confess in our Creed, "The
Son is of the Father alone, not made, nor created, but
begotten."

St. John proceeds :—

" The Word was with God."

In Justin we read :—

" This Offspring, which was truly brought forth from the
Father, was with the Father before all the creatures, and the
Father communed with Him." (Dial. ch. lxii.)

Again, a little before, in the same chapter :—

" From which we can indisputably learn that God conversed with some One who was numerically distinct from
Himself."

Again :—

" The Word, Who also was with Him." (Apol. ii. ch. vi.)

Again, Trypho says :—

" You maintain Him to be pre-existent God." (Ch.
lxxxvii.)

Again :—

" I asserted that this Power was begotten from the Father,
by His Power and Will, but not by abscission, as if the essence
of the Father were divided; as all other things partitioned
and divided are not the same after as before they were
divided; and for the sake of example I took the case of fires
kindled from a fire, which we see to be distinct from it," &c.
(Dial. cxxviii.)

" The Word was God."

Justin writes :—

" The Word of Wisdom, Who is Himself this God begotten of the Father of all things " (Dial. ch. lxi.) (See
previous page.)

Again :—

" They who affirm that the Son is the Father are proved neither to have become acquainted with the Father, nor to know that the Father of the Universe has a Son ; Who also, being the first-begotten Word of God, is even God." (Apol. I. ch. lxiii.)

Again :—

" It must be admitted absolutely that some other One is called Lord by the Holy Spirit besides Him Who is considered Maker of all things." (Dial. ch. lvi.)

But it is useless to multiply quotations, seeing that all those in pages 69-71 are the echoes of this declaration of the Fourth Evangelist.

St. John writes :—

" ALL THINGS WERE MADE BY HIM."

And Justin writes :—

" Knowing that God conceived and made the world by the Word." (Apol. I. ch. lxiv.)

Again :—

" When at first He created and arranged all things by Him." (Apol. II. ch. vi.)

Again St. John writes : —

" THAT (*i. e.* THE WORD) WAS THE TRUE LIGHT THAT LIGHTETH EVERY MAN THAT COMETH INTO THE WORLD."

I have given above (p. 51) sufficient illustrations from Justin of this truth. I again draw attention to :—

" He is the Word of Whom every race of men were partakers." (Apol. I. ch. xlvi.)

Again :—

" He was and is the Word Who is in every man." (Apol. II. ch. x.)

"For whatever either lawgivers or philosophers uttered well, they elaborated by finding and contemplating some part of the Word. But since they did not know the whole of the Word which is Christ, they often contradicted themselves." [1] (Apol. II. ch. x.)

Again :—

"These men who believe in Him, in whom (ἐν οἷς) abideth the seed of God, the Word." (Apol. I. ch. xxxii.)

Again :—

"I confess that I both boast and with all my strength strive to be found a Christian; not because the teachings of Plato are different from those of Christ, but because they are not in all respects similar, as neither are those of the others, Stoics, and poets, and historians. For each man spoke well in proportion to the share he had of the spermatic Word." [2] (Apol. II. ch. xiii.)

Lastly, St. John writes :—

"THE WORD WAS MADE FLESH."

And Justin writes :—

"The Logos Himself, Who took shape and became man and was called Jesus Christ." (Apol. II. ch. v.)

Again :—

"The Word, Who is also the Son; and of Him we will in what follows relate how He took flesh, and became Man." (Apol. II. ch. xxxii.)

"Jesus Christ is the only proper Son Who has been begotten by God, being His Word, and First-begotten, and

---

[1] Dr. Pusey translates this passage thus :—"For all that the philosophers and legislators at any time declared or discovered aright, they accomplished according to their portion of discovery and contemplation of the Word; but as they did not know all the properties of the Word which is Christ, " &c.

[2] Translated by Dr. Pusey, "Seminal Divine Word."

Power, and becoming man according to His Will He taught us these things," &c.   (Apol. i. ch. xxiii.)

Again :—

" In order that you may recognize Him as God coming forth from above, and Man living among men."   (Dial. lxiv.)

Again :—

" He was the Only-begotten of the Father of all things, being begotten in a peculiar manner Word and Power by Him, and having afterwards become Man through the Virgin." (Dial. ch. cv.)

After considering the above extracts, the reader will be able to judge of the truth of some assertions of the author of " Supernatural Religion," as, for instance :—

" We are, in fact, constantly directed by the remarks of Justin to other sources of the Logos doctrine, and never to the Fourth Gospel, with which his tone and terminology in no way agree."   (Vol. ii. p. 293.)

Again :—

" We must see that Justin's terminology, as well as his views of the Word become Man, is thoroughly different from that Gospel."   (Vol. ii. p. 296.)

Also :—

" It must be apparent to every one who seriously examines the subject, that Justin's terminology is thoroughly different from, and in spirit opposed to, that of the Fourth Gospel, and in fact that the peculiarities of the Gospel are not found in Justin's writings at all." (! !) (P. 297.)[1]

---

[1] A few pages further on I shall show that the mode of reasoning adopted by the author of "Supernatural Religion," in drawing inferences from the ways in which Justin expresses the idea of St. John's ὁ λόγος σὰρξ ἐγένετο would, if we adopted it, lead us to some very startling conclusions.

On the contrary, we assert that every Divine Truth respecting the Logos, which appears in the germ in St. John, is expanded in Justin. St. John's short and pithy sentences are the text, and Justin's remarks are the exposition of that text, and of nothing less or more.

So far from Justin's doctrine being contrary to the spirit of St. John's, Justin, whilst deviating somewhat from the strict letter, seizes and reproduces the very spirit. I will give in the next section two or three remarkable instances of this; which instances, strange to say, the author of " Supernatural Religion " quotes for the, purpose of showing the absolute divergence and opposition between the two writers.

THE PRINCIPAL WITNESS ON OUR LORD AS KING, PRIEST, AND ANGEL.

THE author of " Supernatural Religion " quotes the passage in Dial. xxxiv.:—

" For Christ is King, and Priest, and God, and Lord, and Angel, and Man, and Captain, and Stone, and a Son born," &c.

And he remarks, with what I cannot but characterize as astonishing effrontery, or (to use his own language with respect to Tischendorf) " an assurance which can scarcely be characterized otherwise than an unpardonable calculation upon the ignorance of his readers." (Vol. ii. p. 56.)

" Now these representations, which are constantly repeated throughout Justin's writings, are quite opposed to the spirit of the Fourth Gospel." (Vol. ii. p. 288.)

He first of all takes the title " King," and arbitrarily and unwarrantably restricts Justin's derivation of it to the seventy-second Psalm, apparently being ignorant of the fact that St. John, in his very first chapter, records that Christ was addressed by Nathanael as " King of Israel "—that the Fourth Gospel alone describes how the crowd on His entry into Jerusalem cried, " Osanna,

Blessed be the King of Israel, Who cometh in the name of the Lord " (xii. 13)—that this Gospel more fully than any other records how Pilate questioned our Lord respecting His Kingship, and recognized Him as King, " Behold your King ;" and that those who mocked our Lord are recorded by St. John to have mocked Him as the " King of Israel."

So that this term King, so far from being contrary to the spirit of the Fourth Gospel, is not even contrary to its letter.

But this, gross though it seems, is to my mind as nothing to two other assertions founded on this passage of Justin :—

"If we take the second epithet, the Logos as Priest, which is quite foreign to the Fourth Gospel, we find it repeated by Justin."

Now, it is quite true that the title " priest " is not given to our Lord in St. John, just as it is not given to Him in any one of the three Synoptics, or indeed in any book of the New Testament, except the Epistle to the Hebrews : yet, notwithstanding this, of all the books of the New Testament, this Gospel is the one which sets forth the reality of Christ's Priesthood. For what is the distinguishing function of the Priesthood ? Is it not Mediation and Intercession, and the Fourth Gospel more than all sets forth Christ as Mediator and Intercessor ? As Mediator when He says so absolutely: " No man cometh unto the Father but by me ;" " As my Father sent me so send I you ; whosesoever sins ye remit, they are remitted unto them."

Again, the idea of Priesthood is actually inherent in the figure of the good Shepherd " Who giveth His Life for

the sheep;" for how does He give His life?—not in the
way of physical defence against enemies, as an earthly
" good shepherd " might do, but in the way of atoning
Sacrifice, as the author of " Supernatural Religion "
truly asserts, where he writes (vol. ii. p. 352):—

"The representation of Jesus as the Lamb of God taking
away the sins of the world is the very basis of the Fourth
Gospel."

Again, in the same page :—

" He died for the sin of the world, and is the object of
faith, by which alone forgiveness and justification before God
can be secured."

Again, with reference to His Intercession, we have not
only the truth set forth in such expressions as " I will
pray the Father," but we have the actual exercise of the
great act of priestly Intercession, as recorded in the
seventeenth chapter of the Fourth Gospel. If we look
to words only (which the author of " Supernatural
Religion " too often does), then, of course, we allow
that the epithet " priest " is quite foreign not only to the
Fourth Gospel, but to every other book of the New Testament, except the Epistle to the Hebrews ; but if we look
to the things implied in the idea of Priesthood, such as
Mediation and Intercession, in fact Intervention between
God and Man, then we find that the whole New Testament is pervaded with the idea, and it culminates in the
Fourth Gospel.

The next assertion of the author of " Supernatural
Religion " on the same passage betrays still more
ignorance of the contents of St. John's Gospel, and a far
greater eagerness to fasten on a seeming omission of the

letter, and to ignore a pervadence of the spirit. He asserts :—

"It is scarcely necessary to point out that this representation of the Logos as Angel, is not only foreign to, but opposed to, the spirit of the Fourth Gospel." (Vol. ii. p. 293.)

Now just as in the former case we had to ask, "What is the characteristic of the priest ? " so in order to answer this we have only to ask, "What is the characteristic of the angel ? "

An angel is simply "one sent." Such is the meaning of the word both in the Old and New Testament. The Hebrew word מלאך is applied indifferently to a messenger sent by man (see Job i. 14; 1 Sam. xi. 3; 2 Sam. xi. 19-20), and to God's messengers the Holy Angels, that is, the Holy Messengers, the Holy ones sent. And similarly, in the New Testament, the word ἄγγελος is applied to human messengers in Luke vii. 24, ἀπελθόντων δὲ τῶν ἀγγέλων Ἰωάννου, also in Luke ix. 52, and James ii. 25. That the characteristic of the angel is to be "sent" is implied in such common phrases as, "The Lord *sent* His Angel," "I will *send* mine angel," "Are they not all ministering spirits *sent* forth to minister ? " &c.

Now one of the characteristic expressions of the Fourth Gospel—we might almost have said *the* characteristic expression—respecting Jesus, is that He is "sent." To use the noun instead of the verb, He is God's special messenger, His ἄγγελος, sent by Him to declare and to do His will : but this does not imply that He has, or has assumed, the nature of an angel ; just as the application of the same word ἄγγελος to mere human messengers in no way implies that they have any other nature than human nature. Just as men sent their fellow-men as their ἄγγελοι, so God sends One Who, according to Justin, fully partakes of His Nature, to be His ἄγγελος.

This sending of our Lord on the part of His Father is one of the chief characteristics of the Fourth Gospel, and the reader, if he cannot examine this Gospel for himself, comparing it with the others, has only to turn to any concordance, Greek or English, to satisfy himself respecting this matter.

Jesus Christ is said to be " sent of God," *i.e.* to be His ἄγγελος, only once in St. Matthew's Gospel (Matthew x. 40 : " He that receiveth me receiveth Him that sent me "), only once in St. Mark (ix. 37), only twice in St. Luke (ix. 48 ; xx. 13), but in the Fourth Gospel He is said to be sent of God about forty times.[1] In one discourse alone, that in John vi., Jesus asserts no less than six times that He is sent of God, or that God sent Him ; so that the dictum, " This representation of the Logos as angel is not only foreign to, but opposed to, the spirit of the Fourth Gospel," is absolutely contrary to the truth.

---

[1] The following are some instances :—" God sent not His Son into the world to condemn the world." " He Whom God sent."— John iii. 17, 23. " My meat is to do the will of Him that sent me." " Jesus Christ, Whom Thou hast sent." " As my Father sent me, so send I you," &c.

Section XIV.

THE PRINCIPAL WITNESS ON THE DOCTRINE OF THE TRINITY.

THE author of " Supernatural Religion " asserts :—

"The Fourth Gospel proclaims the doctrine of an hypostatic Trinity in a more advanced form than any other writing of the New Testament." [1]

This is hardly true if we consider what is meant by the proclamation of the doctrine of a Trinity.

Such a doctrine can be set forth by inference, or it can be distinctly and broadly stated, as it is, for instance, in the First Article of the Church of England, or in the Creed of St. Athanasius.

The doctrine of the Trinity is set forth by implication in every place in Scripture where the attributes or works of God are ascribed to two other Persons besides The Father. But it is still more directly set forth in those places where the Three Persons are mentioned together as acting conjointly in some Divine Work, or receiving

---

[1] This passage does not occur among the remarks upon Justin Martyr's quotations, but among those on the Clementine Homilies. However, it seems to be used to prove that the Gospel of St. John was published after the writing of the Clementines, which the author seems to think were themselves posterior to Justin.

conjointly some divine honour. In this sense the most explicit declarations of the doctrine of the Trinity are the Baptismal formula at the end of St. Matthew's Gospel, and the "grace," as it is called, at the end of St. Paul's Second Epistle to the Corinthians.

St. John, by asserting in different places the Godhead of the Word, and the Divine Works of the Holy Ghost, implicitly proves the doctrine of the Trinity, but, as far as I can remember, he but twice mentions the Three adorable Persons together : Once in the words, " I will pray the Father and He shall give you another Comforter." And again, " But the Paraclete, which is the Holy Ghost, whom the Father shall send in My name, He shall teach you all things."

Now, in respect of the explicit declaration of the doctrine of the Trinity, the statements of Justin are the necessary[1] developments not only of St. John's statements, but of those of the rest of the New Testament writers.

I have given two passages in page 10.

One of these is in the First Apology, and reads thus:—

"Our teacher of these things is Jesus Christ, Who also was born for this purpose, and was crucified under Pontius

[1] I say the " necessary " developments, because Holy Scripture is given to the Church to be expounded and applied, and in order to this its doctrine must be collected out of many scattered statements, and stated and guarded, and this is its being developed. The Persons, the attributes, and the works of the three Persons of the Godhead are so described in Holy Scripture as Divine, and They are so conjoined in the works of Creation, Providence, and Grace, that we cannot but contemplate Them as associated together, and cannot but draw an impassable gulf between Their existence and that of all creatures, and we cannot but adoringly contemplate Their relations one to another, and hence the necessary development of the Christian dogma as contained in the Creeds.

Pilate, Procurator of Judea in the times of Tiberius Cæsar, and that we reasonably worship Him, having learned that He is the Son of the true God Himself, and holding Him in the Second place, and the Prophetic Spirit in the Third, we will prove." (Apol. I. ch. xiii.)

Again, he endeavours to show that Plato held the doctrine of a Trinity. He is proving that Plato had read the books of Moses:—

" And, as to his speaking of a third, he did this because he read, as we said above, that which was spoken by Moses, ' that the Spirit of God moved over the waters.' For he gives the second place to the Logos which is with God, who he (Plato) said, was placed crosswise in the universe; and the third place to the Spirit who was said to be borne upon the water, saying, 'and the third around the third.'" (Apol. I. ch. lx.)

Now unquestionably, so far as expression of doctrine is concerned, these passages from Justin are the developments of the Johannean statements. The statements in St. John contain, in germ, the whole of what Justin develops; but it is absurd to assert that, after Justin had written the above, it was necessary, in order to bolster up a later, and consequently, in the eyes of Rationalists, a mere human development, to forge a new Gospel, containing nothing like so explicit a declaration of the Trinity as we find in writings which are supposed to precede it, and weighting its doctrinal statements with a large amount of historical matter very difficult, in many cases, to reconcile perfectly with the history in the older Synoptics.

JUSTIN AND ST. JOHN ON THE INCARNATION.

TWO further matters, bearing upon the relations of the doctrine of Justin to that of St. John, must now be considered. The Author of " Supernatural Religion" asserts that the doctrine of Justin respecting the Incarnation of the Word is essentially different from that of St. John :—

" It must be borne in mind that the terminology of John i. 14, 'And the Word became flesh' (σὰρξ ἐγένετο) is different from that of Justin, who uses the word σαρκοποιηθείς." (Vol. ii. p. 276.)

Again, with reference to the word μονογενὴς, he writes :—

" The phrase in Justin is quite different from that in the Fourth Gospel, i. 14, 'And the Word became flesh' (σὰρξ ἐγένετο) 'and tabernacled among us, and we beheld his glory, glory as of the Only-begotten from the Father' (ὡς μονογενοῦς παρὰ πατρὸς, &c.). In Justin He is 'the Only-begotten of the Father of all' (μονογενὴς τῷ Πατρὶ τῶν ὅλων), 'and He became man' (ἄνθρωπος γενόμενος) 'through the Virgin,' and Justin never once employs the peculiar terminology of the Fourth Gospel, σὰρξ ἐγένετο, in any part of his writings." (Vol. ii. p. 280.)

Again :—

" He [Justin] is, in fact, thoroughly acquainted with the history of the Logos doctrine and its earlier enunciation under the symbol of Wisdom, and his knowledge of it is clearly independent of, and antecedent to, the statements of the Fourth Gospel." (Vol. ii. p. 284.)

This passage is important. I think we cannot be wrong in deducing from it that the Author of " Super-natural Religion" considers that the Gospel of St. John was published subsequently to the time of Justin Martyr, that is, some time after A.D. 160 or 165.

Again :—

" The peculiarity of his terminology in all these passages [all which I have given above in pages 73-78], so markedly different, and even opposed to that of the Fourth Gospel, will naturally strike the reader." (Vol. ii. p. 286.)

Again, and lastly :—

" We must see that Justin's terminology, as well as his views of the Word become man, is thoroughly different from that Gospel. We have remarked that, although the passages are innumerable in which Justin speaks of the Word having become man through the Virgin, he never once throughout his writings makes use of the peculiar expression of the Fourth Gospel : ' The word became flesh' (ὁ λόγος σὰρξ ἐγένετο). On the few occasions on which he speaks of the Word having been *made* flesh, he uses the term, σαρκοποιηθείς. In one instance he has σάρκα ἔχειν, and speaking of the Eucharist, Justin once explains that it is in memory of Christ being made *body*, σωματοποιήσασθαι. Justin's most common phrase, however, and he repeats it in numberless instances, is that the Logos submitted to be born, and become man (γεννηθῆναι ἄνθρωπον γενόμενον ὑπέμεινεν), by a Virgin, or he uses variously the expressions : ἄνθρωπος γέγονε, ἄνθρωπος γενόμενος, γενέσθαι ἄνθρωπον." (Vol. ii. p. 296.)

Here, then, we have the differences specified by which the Author of "Supernatural Religion" thinks that he is justified in describing the terminology and views of Justin respecting the Incarnation as "markedly different and even opposed to," and as "thoroughly different from," those of the Fourth Gospel.

So that, because Justin, instead of embodying the sentence, ὁ λόγος σὰρξ ἐγένετο, substitutes for it the participle, σαρκοποιηθεὶς, or the phrase, σάρκα ἔχειν, or the infinitive, σωματοποιήσασθαι, or the expression, ἄνθρωπος γέγονε, he holds views thoroughly different from those of St. John respecting the most momentous of Christian truths.

This is a fair specimen of the utterly reckless assertions in which this author indulges respecting the foundation truth of Christianity.

If such terms, implying such divergences, can be applied to these statements of Justin's *belief* in the Incarnation, what words of human language could be got to express his flat denial of the truth held in common by him and by St. John, if he had been an unbeliever? If Justin, with most other persons, considers that being "in the flesh" is the characteristic difference between men and spirits such as the angels, and expresses himself accordingly by saying that the Word "became man," what sense is there in saying that he is "opposed to the spirit of the Fourth Gospel," in which we have the Word not only as the "Son of Man," but possessing all the sinless weaknesses of human nature, so that He is weary, and weeps, and groans, and is troubled in spirit?

And now we will make, if the reader will allow, a supposition analogous to some which the author of "Super-

natural Religion" has made in pages 360 and following
of his first volume. We will suppose that all the ecclesiastical literature, inspired and uninspired, previous to
the Council of Nice, had been blotted out utterly, and
the Four Gospels alone preserved. And we will suppose
some critic taking upon himself to argue that the Gospel
of St. John was written after the Nicene Creed. On the
principles and mode of argument of the author of " Supernatural Religion," he would actually be able to prove his
absurdity, for he would be able to allege that the doctrine
and terminology of the Fathers of the first General
Council was " opposed to " that of the Fourth Gospel;
and so they could not possibly have acknowledged its
authority if they had even " seen " it. For he (the
critic) would allege that the words of St. John respecting the Incarnation are not adopted by the Creed which
the Nicene Fathers put forth; instead of inserting into
the Creed the words ὁ λόγος σὰρξ ἐγένετο, which, the critic
would urge, they *must have done* if they would success-
fully oppose foes who appealed to the letter of Scripture,
they used other terms, as the participles σαρκωθέντα and
ἐνανθρωπήσαντα.[1] Again, the supposed critic would
urge, they applied to our Lord the phrase γεννηθέντα
πρὸ πάντων τῶν αἰώνων, a phrase " so markedly different
and indeed opposed to that of the Fourth Gospel," as the
author of " Supernatural Religion" urges with respect to
γέννημα πρὸ πάντων τῶν ποιημάτων, and ἀπὸ τοῦ Πατρὸς
τῶν ὅλων γεννηθείς. Again, the critic would urge that

---

[1] Τὸν δι' ἡμᾶς τοὺς ἀνθρώπους καὶ διὰ τὴν ἡμετέραν σωτηρίαν
κατελθόντα ἐκ τῶν οὐρανῶν, καὶ σαρκωθέντα ἐκ Πνεύματος Ἁγίου
καὶ Μαρίας τῆς παρθένου, καὶ ἐνανθρωπήσαντα, κ.τ.λ.

instead of calling the Son "God" absolutely, as in the sentence "the Word was God," they confess Him only as Θεὸς ἐκ Θεοῦ, and this because He is γεννηθείς, and so he would say, with the author of "Supernatural Religion," "This is a totally different view from that of the Fourth Gospel, which in so emphatic a manner enunciates the doctrine, 'In the beginning was the Word, and the Word was with God, and God was the Word;'" and so our supposed critic will exclaim, "See what abundant proof that these Fathers had 'never even seen' the Fourth Gospel;" and according to all rules of Rationalistic criticism they had not, or, at least, they thought nothing of its authenticity; whilst all the time this same Gospel was open before them, and they devoutly reverenced every word as the word of the Holy Ghost, and would have summarily anathematized any one who had expressed the smallest doubt respecting its plenary Inspiration.

JUSTIN AND ST. JOHN ON THE SUBORDINATION OF THE SON.

THE second matter connected with the relations of the doctrine of Justin Martyr to that of St. John, is the subordination of the Son to the Father.

I have already noticed this truth (page 49), but, owing to its importance it may be well to devote to it a few further remarks. The author of " Supernatural Religion " does not seem to realize that in perfect Sonship two things are inherent, viz., absolute sameness (and therefore equality) of nature with the Father, and perfect subordination in the submission of His will to that of the Father.

He consequently asserts :——

" It is certain, however, that both Justin and Philo, unlike the prelude to the Fourth Gospel, place the Logos in a secondary position to God the Father, another point indicating a less advanced stage of the doctrine. Both Justin and Philo apply the term θεὸς to the Logos without the article. Justin distinctly says, that Christians worship Jesus Christ as the Son of the True God, holding Him in the Second Place (ἐν δευτέρᾳ χώρᾳ ἔχοντες), and this secondary position is systematically defined through Justin's writings in a very decided way, as it is in the works of Philo, by the contrast of the begotten Logos with the unbegotten God. Justin speaks of the Word as the 'first born of the unbegotten God' (πρωτότοκος τῷ ἀγεννήτῳ Θεῷ), and the distinctive appellation of the 'unbegotten God,' applied to the Father, is most common in all his writings." (Vol. ii. p. 291.)

Now, when Justin speaks of holding Christ "in the Second Place," he does no more nor less than any Trinitarian Christian of the present day, when such an one speaks of the Son as the *Second* Person of the Trinity, and as the only begotten Son and the Word of the Father.

When we speak of Him as being the Second Person, we necessarily rank Him in the second place in point of numerical order. When we speak of Him as being the Son, we naturally place Him as, in the order of conception, second to, or after, Him that begat Him;[1] and, when we speak of Him as the Word, we also place Him in order of conception as after Him Who utters or gives forth the Word.

Justin says no more than this in any expression which he uses.

When he speaks of the Father as the unbegotten God, and the Son as the Begotten God, he does no more than the most uncompromising believer in the doctrine of the ever-blessed Trinity in the present day does, when, in the words of the Creed of St. Athanasius, that believer confesses that

" The Father is made of none, neither created nor begotten.

---

[1] Though of course not as regards *time*, for all Catholics hold the Eternal Generation, that there never was a time in which the Father was not a Father ; nor as regards power or extension, for whatever the Father does that the Son does also, and wherever the Father is there is the Son also.

" The Son is of the Father alone, neither made, nor created, but begotten."

But we have not now so much to do with the orthodoxy of Justin as with the question as to whether his
doctrine is anterior to St. John's, as being less decided
in its assertions of our Lord's equality.

Now there are no words in Justin on the side of our
Lord's subordination at all equal to the words of Christ
as given in St. John, " My Father is greater than I."

The Gospel of St. John is pervaded by two great
truths which underlie every part, and are the necessary
complements of one another; these are, the perfect
equality or identity of the nature of the Son with that of
the Father, because He is the true begotten Son of His
Father; and the perfect submission of the Will of the
Son to that of the Father because He is His Father.

The former appears in such assertions as " The Word
was with God," " The Word was God," " My Lord and
My God," " I and the Father are one," " He that hath
seen Me hath seen the Father," " The glory which I had
with Thee before the world was," " All things that the
Father hath are mine," &c.

The latter is inherent in the idea of perfect Sonship,
and is asserted in such statements as

God " gave His only begotten Son" (iii. 16).

" The Father loveth the Son, and hath given all
things into His hands" (iii. 35).

" The Son can do nothing of Himself" (v. 19).

" The Father loveth the Son, and showeth Him all
things that Himself doeth " (v. 20).

The Father hath " given to the Son to have life in
Himself" (v. 26).

The Father " hath given Him authority to execute judgment also " (v. 27).

" I seek not mine own will, but the will of the Father" (v. 30).

" The works which the Father hath given me to finish " (v. 36).

" I am come in my Father's name " (v. 43).

" Him [the Son of Man] hath God the Father sealed " (vi. 27).

" I live by the Father " (v. 57).

" My doctrine is not mine, but His that sent me " (vii. 16).

" He that seeketh His glory that sent Him, the same is true " (vii. 18).

" I am from Him, and He hath sent me " (vii. 29).

" I do nothing of myself, but as my Father hath taught me, I speak these things " (viii. 28).

" Neither came I of myself, but He sent me " (viii. 42).

" I have power to take it [my life] again ; this commandment have I received of my Father " (x. 18).

"My Father, which gave them me, is greater than all " (x. 29).

" I have kept my Father's commandments, and abide in His love " (xv. 10).

I have read Justin carefully for the purpose of marking every expression in his writings bearing upon the relations of the Son to the Father, and I find none so strongly expressing subordination as these, and the declarations of this kind in the works of Justin are nothing like so numerous as they are in the short Gospel of St. John.

The reader who knows anything about the history of Christian doctrine will see at a glance how impossible it

would have been for a Gospel ascribing these expressions
to Jesus to have been received by the Christian Church
long before Justin's time, except that Gospel had been
fully authenticated as the work of the last surviving
Apostle.

JUSTIN AND PHILO.

THE writer of "Supernatural Religion" asserts that Justin derived his Logos doctrine from Philo, and also that his doctrine was identical with that of Philo and opposed to that of St. John.

But respecting this assertion two questions may be asked.

From whom did Philo derive *his* doctrine of the Logos? and

From whom did Justin derive his identification of the Logos with Jesus?

The Christian, all whose conceptions of salvation rest ultimately upon the truth that "The Word was God," believes (if, that is, he has any knowledge of the history of human thought), that God prepared men for the reception of so momentous a truth long before that truth was fully revealed. He believes that God prepared the Gentiles for the reception of this truth by familiarizing them with some idea of the Logos through the speculations of Plato; and he also believes that God prepared His chosen people for receiving the same truth by such means as the personification of Wisdom in the book of Proverbs, and in the Apocryphal moral books, and, above all, by the identification of the active presence and power of God with the Meymera or Word, as set forth in the Chaldee paraphrases.

Both these lines of thought seem to have coalesced and to have reached their full development (so far as they could, at least, apart from Christianity) in Alexandrian Judaism, which is principally known to us in the pages of Philo ; but how much of Philo's own speculation is contained in the extracts from his writings given by the author of " Supernatural Religion" it is impossible to say, as we know very little of the Alexandrian Jewish literature except from him. He seems, however, to write as if what he enunciated was commonly known and accepted by those for whom he wrote.

There are two reasons which make me think that Justin, if he derived any part of his Logos doctrines from Alexandrian sources (which I much doubt), derived them from writings or traditions to which Philo, equally with himself, was indebted.

One is that, in his Dialogue with Trypho, a Jew, he never mentions Philo, whose name would have been a tower of strength to him in disputing with a Jew, and convincing him that there might be another Person Who might be rightly called God besides the Father.

Surely if Justin had known that Philo had spoken of God

" Appointing His true Logos, his first begotten Son, to have the care of this sacred flock as the substitute of the great King " (quoted in p. 274);

and that—

" The most ancient Word is the image of God " (p. 274) ;

and that

" The Word is the image of God by which the whole world was created " (p. 275) ;

surely, I say, he would have used the name of one who had been in his day such a champion of the Jewish people, and had suffered such insults from Caligula on their account.[1]

Nothing seems more appropriate for the conversion of Trypho than many of the extracts from Philo given by the author of " Supernatural Religion." Herein, too, in this matter of Philo and Justin, the author of " Supernatural Religion " betrays his surprising inconsistency and refutes himself. He desires it to be inferred that Justin need not have seen—probably had not seen, even one of our present Gospels, because he does not name the authors, though there is abundant reason why the names of four authors of the Memoirs should not be paraded before unbelievers as suggesting differences in the testimony ; whereas it would have been the greatest assistance to him in his argument with Trypho to have named Philo ; and he does not. We would not infer from this, as the author of " Supernatural Religion " does most absurdly in parallel cases, that Justin " knew nothing " of Philo ; had not even seen his books, and need not have heard of him ; but we must gather from it that Justin did not associate the name of Philo with the Logos doctrine in its most advanced stage of development. Many other facts tend to show that Justin made little or no use of Philo. In the extracts given by the author of " Supernatural Religion " from

---

[1] Eusebius, B. ii. ch. v.

Philo, all culled out to serve his purpose, the reader will notice many words and phrases " foreign " to Justin ; for instance, δεύτερος Θεός, ὄργανον δὲ Λόγον Θεοῦ, δι' οὗ σύμπας ὁ κόσμος ἐδημιουργεῖτο. More particularly the reader will notice that such adjectives as ὀρθὸς, ἱερὸς (ἱερώτατος) and πρέσβυς (πρεσβύτατος) are applied to the Word in the short extracts from Philo given by the author of " Supernatural Religion," which are never applied to the Second Person of the Trinity in Justin. In fact, though there are some slight resemblances, the terminology of Philo is, to use the words of " Supernatural Religion," " totally different from " and " opposed to " that of Justin, and the more closely it is examined, the more clearly it will be seen that Justin cannot have derived his Logos doctrine from Philo.

The other question is, " from whom did Justin derive his identification of the Logos with Jesus ? "

Not from Philo, certainly. We have shown above how St. John lays down with authority the identity of the Logos with the pre-existent Divine Nature of Jesus, not in long, elaborate, carefully reasoned philosophical dissertation, but in four short, clear, decisive enunciations. " In the beginning was the Word "—" The Word was with God "—" The Word was God "—" The Word was made flesh."

We have seen how these were the manifest germs of Justin's teaching. Now, if at the time when Justin wrote, the Fourth Gospel, as we shall shortly prove, must have been in use in the Church in every part of the world, why should Justin be supposed to derive from Philo a truth which he, being a Jew, would repudiate ? Justin himself most certainly was not the first to identify the Logos with Jesus. The identification was asserted long before in the Apocalypse, which the author of " Supernatural Religion " shows to have been written about A. D. 70, or so. In fact, he ascertains its date to " a few weeks." Supposing, then, that the Apocalypse was anterior to St. John, on whose lines, so to speak, does Justin develope the Logos doctrine ? Most assuredly not on Philo's lines (for his whole terminology essentially differs from that of the Alexandrian), but on the lines of the fourth Gospel, and on no other.

Let the reader turn to some extracts which the author of " Supernatural Religion " gives out of Philo. In p. 265, he gives some very striking passages indeed, in which Philo speaks of the Logos as the Bread from heaven :—

" He is ' the substitute ($ὕπαρχος$) of God,' ' the heavenly incorruptible food of the soul,' ' the bread from heaven.' In one place he says, ' and they who inquire what nourishes the soul . . . . learnt at last that it is the Word of God, and the Divine Reason' . . . . This is the heavenly nourishment to which the Holy Scripture refers . . . . saying, ' Lo I rain upon you bread ($ἄρτος$) from heaven' (Exod. xvi. 4). ' This is the bread ($ἄρτος$) which the Lord has given them to eat.' " (Exod. xvi. 15.)

And again :—

" For the one indeed raises his eyes to the sky, perceiving the Manna, the Divine Word, the heavenly incorruptible food of the longing soul." Elsewhere . . . . " but it is taught by the initiating priest and prophet Moses, who declares, ' This is the bread ($ἄρτος$), the nourishment which God has given to the soul.' His own Reason and His own Word which He has offered; for this bread ($ἄρτος$) which He has given us to eat is Reason." (Vol. ii. p. 265.)

Now the Fourth Gospel also makes Jesus speak of Himself as the "Bread of Life," and "given by the Father;" but what is the bread defined by Jesus Himself to be? Not a mere intellectual apprehension, *i.e.* Reason, as Philo asserts; but the very opposite, no other than "His Flesh;" the product of His Incarnation. "The bread that I will give is My Flesh," and He adds to it His Blood. "Except ye eat the Flesh of the Son of Man and drink His Blood, ye have no life in you."

Now this also Justin reproduces, not after the conception of Philo, which is but a natural conception, but after the conception of Jesus in the Fourth Gospel, which is an infinitely mysterious and supernatural one.

"In like manner as Jesus Christ our Saviour, having been made flesh by the Word of God, had both flesh and blood for our Salvation, so likewise have we been taught that the food which is blessed by the prayer of His Word, and from which our blood and flesh are by transmutation nourished is the Flesh and Blood of that Jesus Who was made flesh." (Apol. I. ch. lxvi.)

I trust the reader will acquit me, in making this quotation, of any desire to enunciate any Eucharistic theory of the presence of Christ's Flesh in the Eucharist. All I have to do with is the simple fact that both Philo and St. John speak of the Word as the Bread of Life; but Philo explains that bread to be "reason," and St. John makes our Lord to set it forth as His Flesh, and Justin takes no notice of the idea of Philo, and reproduces the idea of the fourth Gospel.

And yet we are to be told that Justin "knew nothing" of the Fourth Gospel, and that his Logos doctrine was "identical" with that of Philo.

DISCREPANCIES BETWEEN ST. JOHN AND THE SYNOPTICS.

THE author of "Supernatural Religion" devotes a large portion of his second volume to setting forth the discrepancies, real or alleged, between the Synoptics and the Fourth Gospel.

In many of these remarks he seems to me to betray extraordinary ignorance of the mere contents of the Fourth Gospel. I shall notice two or three remarkable misconceptions; but, before doing this, I desire to call the reader's attention to the only inference respecting the authorship of this Gospel which can be drawn from these discrepancies.

St. John's Gospel is undoubtedly the last Gospel published; in fact, the last work of the sacred canon. The more patent, then, the differences between St. John and the Synoptics, the more difficult it is to believe that a Gospel, containing subject-matter so different from the works already accepted as giving a true account of Christ, should have been accepted by the whole Church at so comparatively recent a date, unless that Church had every reason for believing that it was the work of the last surviving Apostle.

Take, for instance, the [apparent] differences between

St. John and the Synoptics respecting the scene of our Lord's ministry, the character of His discourses, the miracles ascribed to Him, and the day of His Crucifixion, or rather of His partaking of the Paschal feast. The most ignorant and unobservant would notice these differences; and the more labour required to reconcile the statements or representations of the last Gospel with the three preceding ones, the more certain it is that none would have ventured to put forth a document containing such differences except an Apostle who, being the last surviving one, might be said to inherit the prestige and authority of the whole college.

It would far exceed the limits which I have prescribed to myself to examine the Fourth Gospel with the view of reconciling the discrepancies between it and the Synoptics, and also of bringing out the numberless undesigned coincidences between the earlier and the later account, of which the writer of " Supernatural Religion," led away by his usual dogmatic prejudices, has taken not the smallest notice.

The reader will find this very ably treated in Mr. Sanday's " Authorship of the Fourth Gospel" (Macmillan).

My object at present is of a far humbler nature, simply to show the utter untrustworthiness of some of the most confidently asserted statements of the writer of " Supernatural Religion."

I shall take two:

1. The difference between Christ's mode of teaching and the structure of His discourses, as represented by St. John and the Synoptics respectively.

2. The intellectual impossibility that St. John should have written the Fourth Gospel.

1. Respecting the difference of Christ's mode of teaching as recorded in St. John and in the Synoptics, he remarks :—

"It is impossible that Jesus can have had two such diametrically opposed systems of teaching; one purely moral, the other wholly dogmatic; one expressed in wonderfully terse, clear, brief sayings and parables, the other in long, involved, and diffuse discourses; one clothed in the great language of humanity, the other concealed in obscure, philosophic terminology; and that these should have been kept so distinct as they are in the Synoptics, on the one hand, and the Fourth Gospel on the other. The tradition of Justin Martyr applies solely to the system of the Synoptics, ' Brief and concise were the sentences uttered by Him: for He was no Sophist, but His word was the power of God.'"[1] (Vol. ii. p. 468.)

To take the first of these assertions. So far from its being "impossible" that Jesus " can have had two such diametrically opposite modes of teaching," it is not only possible, but we have undeniable proof of the fact in that remarkable saying of Christ recorded by both St. Matthew and St. Luke : " All things are delivered unto Me of My Father, and no man knoweth the Son, but the Father; neither knoweth any man the Father, save the Son, and he to whomsoever the Son will reveal Him " (Matth. xi. 27). The author of " Supernatural Religion " has studied the letter of this passage very carefully, for he devotes no less than ten pages to a minute examination of the supposed quotations of it in Justin and other Fathers (vol. i. pp. 402-412); but he does not draw attention to the fact that it is conceived in the spirit and

---

[1] Apol. i. 14.

expressed in the terms of the Fourth Gospel, and totally unlike the general style of the discourses in the Synoptics.[1] The Fourth Gospel shows us that such words as these, almost unique in the Synoptics, are not the only words uttered in a style so different from the usual teaching of our Lord—that at times, when He was on the theme of His relations to His Father, He adopted other diction more suited to the nature of the deeper truths He was enunciating.

Then take the second assertion :—

" One [system] expressed in wonderfully terse, clear, brief sayings and parables, the other in long, involved, and diffuse discourses."

Again :—

" The description which Justin gives of the manner of teaching of Jesus excludes the idea that he knew the Fourth Gospel. 'Brief and concise were the sentences uttered by Him, for He was no Sophist, but His word was the power of God.' (Apol. I. 14.) No one could for a moment assert that this description applies to the long and artificial discourses of the Fourth Gospel, whilst, on the other hand, it eminently describes the style of teaching with which we are acquainted in the Synoptics, with which the Gospel according to the Hebrews, in all its forms, was so closely allied." (Vol. ii. p. 315.)

Now I assert, and the reader can with very little trouble verify the truth of the assertion, that the mode of our Lord's teaching, as set forth in St. John, is more terse, axiomatic, and sententious—more in accordance

---

[1] The spirit of this verse, and its form of expression, are quite those of the Gospel of St. John; and it serves to form a link of union between the three Synoptic Gospels and the Fourth, and to point to the vast and weighty mass of discourses of the Lord which are not related except by St. John. Alford in loco.

with these words of Justin, "brief and concise were the sentences uttered by Him," than it appears in the Synoptics.

To advert for a moment to the mere length of the discourses. The Sermon on the Mount is considerably longer than the longest discourse in St. John's Gospel (viz., that occupying chapters xiv., xv., xvi.). This is the only unbroken discourse of any length in this Gospel. The others, viz., those with Nicodemus, with the woman at Sychem, with the Jews in the Temple, and the one in the Synagogue at Capernaum, are much shorter than many in the Synoptics, and none of them are continuous discourses, but rather conversations. And, with respect to the composition, those in St. John are mainly made up of short, terse, axiomatic deliverances just such as Justin describes.

Take, for instance, the sentences in the sixth chapter:—

"I am the bread of life."

"He that believeth on me hath everlasting life."

"I am that bread of life."

"This is the bread that cometh down from heaven, that a man should eat thereof and not die."

"My flesh is meat indeed, and my blood is drink indeed."

"It is the spirit that quickeneth, the flesh profiteth nothing."

And those in the tenth :—

"I am the door of the sheep."

"I am the good shepherd: the good shepherd giveth his life for the sheep."

"I am the good shepherd, and know my sheep, and am known of mine."

Then, if we compare parables, the passage in the Fourth Gospel most resembling a parable, viz., the similitude of the Vine and the branches, is made up of detached sentences more " terse" and " concise" than those of most parables in the Synoptics.

The discourses in St. John are upon subjects very distasteful to the author of " Supernatural Religion," and he loses no opportunity of expressing his dislike to them; but it is a gross misrepresentation to say that the instruction, whatever it be, is conveyed in other than sentences as simple, terse, and concise as those of the Synoptics, though the subject-matter is different.

We will now proceed to the last assertion :—

" One [system of teaching] clothed in the great language of humanity, the other concealed in obscure philosophic terminology."

What can this writer mean by the " philosophic terminology " of our Lord's sayings as reported in the Fourth Gospel ? If the use of the term " Logos " be " philosophio terminology," it is confined to four sentences; and these not the words of Jesus Himself, but of the Evangelist. I do not remember throughout the rest of the Gospel a single sentence which can be properly called " philosophical."

The author must confound " philosophical " with " mysterious." Each and every discourse in the fourth Gospel is upon, or leads to, some deep mystery; but that mystery is in no case set forth in philosophical, but in what the author of " Supernatural Religion " calls the " great language of humanity." Take the most mysterious by far of all the enunciations in St. John's Gospel,

" Except ye eat the flesh of the Son of Man, and drink His Blood, ye have no life in you." What are the words of which this sentence is composed? " Eat," " flesh," " blood," " Son of man," " life."   Are not these the commonest words of daily life ? but, then, their use and association here is the very thing which constitutes the mystery.

Again, take the salient words of each discourse— " Except a man be born again "—" be born of water and of the Spirit." " Whosoever drinketh of the water that I shall give him shall never thirst." " As the Father hath life in Himself, so hath He given to the Son to have life in Himself." " All that are in the graves shall hear His voice and shall come forth." " The bread that I will give is My flesh." " If ye believe not that I am He, ye shall die in your sins." " As the Father knoweth Me, even so know I the Father." " I am the Resurrection and the Life." " Whatsoever ye shall ask in My name, that will I do." " If I go not away, the Comforter will not come unto you : but, if I depart, I will send Him unto you."

It is the deepest of all mysteries that one in flesh and blood can say such things of Himself; but it is a perversion of language to speak of these sayings as " philosophical terminology." They are in a different sphere from all mere *human* philosophy, and, indeed, are opposed to every form of it. Philosophy herself requires a new birth before she can so much as see them.

I must recur, however, to the author's first remark, in which he characterizes the discourses of the Synoptics as " purely moral," and those of St. John as " wholly dogmatic." This is by no means true. The discourses in the Synoptics are on moral subjects, but they continually make dogmatic assertions or implications as pronounced as those in the Fourth Gospel. In the Sermon on the Mount, for instance, the preacher authoritatively adds to and modifies the teaching of the very Decalogue itself. " Ye have heard that it was said το them of old time " (for so ἐρρέθη τοῖς ἀρχαίοις must properly be translated) ; " but I say unto you." Again, Jesus assumes in the same discourse to be the Object of worship and the Judge of quick and dead, and that His recognition is salvation itself, when He says, " Not every one that saith unto Me Lord, Lord, shall enter," &c. " Many shall say to me in that day, Lord, Lord," &c., "then will I profess unto them, I never knew you, depart from me all ye that work iniquity."

Take the following expressions out of a number of similar ones in St. Matthew :—

" I will make you (ignorant fishermen) fishers of men " (implying, I will give you power over souls such as no philosopher or leader of men has had before you). (iv. 21.)

" Blessed are ye when men shall persecute you for My sake." (v. 11.)

" If they have called the master of the house (*i. e.* Jesus) Beelzebub, how much more shall they call them of His household." (x. 25.)

" He that loveth father or mother more than Me is not worthy of me " (so that the holiest of human ties are to give way to His personal demands on the human heart). (x. 37.)

" He that loseth his life for My sake shall find it." (x. 39.)

" No man knoweth the Son, but the Father." (xi. 27.)

" In this place is One greater than the temple."
(xii. 6.)

" The Son of man is Lord even of the Sabbath Day."
(xii. 8.)

" In His (Christ's) Name shall the Gentiles trust."
(xii. 21.)

" In the time of harvest I will say to the reapers," *i. e.*
the angels. (xiii. 30.)

" The Son of man shall send forth his angels." (xiii.
41.)

" I will give unto Thee the keys of the kingdom of
heaven." (xvi. 19.)

" Where two or three are gathered together in My
Name there am I in the midst of them." (xviii. 21.)

" He, [God], sent His servants—He sent other servants—Last of all He sent unto them His Son, saying,
they will reverence My Son." (xxi. 37.)

These places assert, by implication, the highest
dogma respecting the Person of Christ. Who is He
Who has such power in heaven and earth that He commands the angels in heaven, and gives the keys of the
kingdom of God to His servant on earth? What Son is
this Whom none but the Father knoweth, and Who alone
knoweth the Father, and Who reveals the Father to
whomsoever He will? What Son is this compared with
Whom such saints as Moses, David, Elijah, Isaiah, and
Daniel are " servants?" These dogmatic assertions of
the first Gospel suggest the question; and the Fourth
Gospel gives the full and perfect answer—that He is the
Word with God, that He is God, and the Only-begotten
of the Father. The Epistles assume the answer where
one speaks of " Jesus, who, being in the form of God,

thought it not a thing to be tenaciously grasped to be equal with God," and another speaks of God's own Son. and another compares Moses the servant with Christ the Son; but the fullest revelation is reserved to the last Gospel. And herein the order of God's dealings is observed, Who gives the lesser revelation to prepare for the fuller and more perfect. The design of the Gospel is to restore men to the image of God by revealing to them God Himself. But, before this can be done, they must be taught what goodness is, their very moral sense must be renewed. Hence the moral discourses of the Synoptics. Till this foundation is laid, first in the world, and then in the soul, the Gospel has nothing to lay hold of and to work upon; so it was laid first in the Sermon on the Mount, which, far beyond all other teaching, stops every mouth and brings in all the world guilty before God; and then the way is prepared for fuller revelations, such as that of the Atonement by the Death of Christ as set forth in the Epistles of St. Peter and St. Paul, and the revelation culminates in the knowledge of the Father and the Son in the Fourth Gospel.

With respect to the assertion of the author of " Supernatural Religion," that the discourses in this Gospel are, as compared with those in the Synoptics, *wholly* dogmatic, as opposed to moral, the reader may judge of the truth of this by the following sayings of the Fourth Gospel :—

" Every one that doeth evil hateth the light."

" He that doeth truth cometh to the light."

" God is a Spirit, and they who worship Him must worship Him in spirit and in truth."

" They that have done good [shall come forth] to the Resurrection of Life."

" How can ye believe who receive honour one of another, and seek not the honour that cometh of God only ? "

" If any man will do His will, he shall know of the doctrine whether it be of God."

" The truth shall make you free," coupled with

" Whosoever committeth sin is the servant of sin."

" If I your Lord and Master have washed your feet, ye ought also to wash one another's feet."

" A new commandment I give unto you, that ye love one another as I have loved you."

" He that hath My commandments and keepeth them, he it is that loveth Me."

These sayings, the reader will perceive, embody the deepest and highest moral teaching conceivable.

One more point remains to be considered — the impossibility that St. John, taking into account his education and intellect, should have been the author of the Fourth Gospel. This is stated in the following passage :—

" The philosophical statements with which the Gospel commences, it will be admitted, are anything but characteristic of the son of thunder, the ignorant and unlearned fisherman of Galilee, who, to a comparatively late period of life, continued preaching in his native country to his brethren of the circumcision. . . . . In the Alexandrian philosophy, everything was prepared for the final application of the doctrine, and nothing is more clear than the fact that the writer of the Fourth Gospel was well acquainted with the teaching of the Alexandrian school, from which he derived his philosophy, and its elaborate and systematic application to Jesus alone indicates a late development of Christian doctrine, which, we maintain, could not have been attained by the Judaistic son of Zebedee." (Vol. ii. p. 415.)

Again, in the preceding page :—

"Now, although there is no certain information as to the time when, if ever, the Apostle removed into Asia Minor, it is pretty certain that he did not leave Palestine before A.D. 60. · · · . If we consider the Apocalypse to be his work, we find positive evidence of such markedly different thought and language actually existing when the Apostle must have been at least sixty or seventy years of age, that it is quite impossible to conceive that he could have subsequently acquired the language and mental characteristics of the Fourth Gospel."

This, though written principally with reference to the diction, applies still more to the philosophy of the author of the Fourth Gospel. And, indeed, from his using the words "mental characteristics," we have no doubt that he desires such an application.

Now, what are the facts? We must assume that St. John, though "unlearned and ignorant," compared with the leaders of the Jewish commonwealth, at the commencement of his thirty years' sojourn in the Jewish capital, was a man of average intellect. Here, then, we have a member of a sect more aggressive than any before known in the promulgation of its opinions, taking the lead in the teaching and defence of these opinions in a city to which the Jews of all nationalities resorted periodically to keep the great feasts. If the holding of any position would sharpen a man's natural intellect and give him a power over words, and a mental grasp of ideas to which in youth he had been a stranger, that position would be the leading one he held in the Church of such a city as Jerusalem.

In the course of the thirty years which, according to the author of " Supernatural Religion," he lived there, he must have constantly had intercourse with Alexandrian Jews and Christians. It is as probable as not that during this period he had had converse with Philo himself, for the distance between Jerusalem and Alexandria was comparatively trifling. At Pentecost there were present Jews and proselytes from Egypt and the parts of Libya about Cyrene. There was also a Synagogue of the Alexandrians. Now I assert that a few hours' conversation with any Alexandrian Jew, or with any Christian convert from Alexandrian Judaism, would have, *humanly speaking*, enabled the Apostle, even if he knew not a word of the doctrine before, to write the four sentences in which are contained the whole Logos expression of the Fourth Gospel.

St. John must have been familiar with the teaching of traditional interpretation respecting the Meymera as contained in the Chaldee paraphrases; indeed, the more "unlearned" and "ignorant" he was, the more he must have relied upon the Chaldee paraphrases for the knowledge of the Old Testament, the Hebrew having been for centuries a dead language. We have a Chaldee paraphrase of great antiquity on so early and familiar a chapter as the third of Genesis, explaining the voice of the Lord God by the voice of the Meymera, or Word of the Lord God (Genesis iii.).

The natural rendering of this word into Greek would be Logos. I repeat, then, that, humanly speaking, if he had never entertained the idea before, a very short conversation with an Alexandrian Jew would have furnished him with all the "philosophy" required to make the four statements in which he simply identifies the Logos with the Divine Nature of his Lord.

Of course, I do not for a moment believe that the Apostle was enabled to write the exordium of his Gospel by any such inspiration. There is not a more direct utterance of the Holy Spirit in all Scripture than that which we have in the prelude to the Fourth Gospel.

But in the eyes of a Christian the grace of the Holy Spirit is shown in the power and explicitness, and above all in the simplicity of the assertions which identify the human conception, if such it can be called, of Platonism, or Judaism, with the highest divine truth.

I believe that if the Apostle wrote these sentences at the time handed down by the Church's tradition, that is, when Cerinthian and other heresies respecting our Lord's nature were beginning to be felt, the power of the Holy Spirit was put forth to restrict him to these few simple utterances, and to restrain his human intellect from overloading them with philosophical or controversial applications of them, which would have marred their simplicity and diminished their power.[1]

---

[1] If the reader desires to see Logos doctrine expressed in philosophic terminology, he can find it in some of the extracts from Philo given in the notes of "Supernatural Religion," vol. ii. pp. 272-298. Can there be a greater contrast than that between St. John's terse, concise, simple, enunciations and the following :—Καὶ οὐ μόνον φῶς, ἀλλὰ καὶ παντὸς ἑτέρου φωτὸς ἀρχέτυπον μᾶλλον δὲ ἀρχετύπου πρεσβύτερον καὶ ἀνώτερον, Λόγον ἔχον παραδείγματος τὸ μὲν γὰρ παράδειγμα ὁ πληρέστατος ἦν αὐτοῦ Λόγος, κ. τ. λ.— De Somniis, i. 15, Mang. i. 634. There is no particularly advanced philosophic terminology here, and yet there is a profound difference between both the thought and wording of this sentence of Philo and St. John's four enunciations of the Logos. Again, Δῆλον δὲ ὅτι καὶ ἡ ἀρχέτυπος σφραγὶς, ὃν φάμεν εἶναι κόσμον νοητὸν, αὐτὸς ἂν εἴη τὸ ἀρχέτυπον παράδειγμα, ἰδέα τῶν ἰδεῶν, ὁ Θεοῦ Λόγος.— De Mundi Opificio Mang. vol. i. p. 8. "It is manifest also that the archetypal seal, which we call that world which is perceptible only to the intellect, must itself be the archetypal model, the idea of ideas, the word of God." (Yonge's Translation.)

EXTERNAL PROOFS OF THE AUTHENTICITY OF OUR FOUR GOSPELS.

WE have now shown that Justin Martyr, the principal witness brought forward by the author of "Supernatural Religion" to discredit the Four Evangelists, either made use of the very books which we now possess, or books which contain exactly the same information respecting our Lord's miraculous 'Birth, Death, Resurrection, and moral teaching. We have seen, also, that Justin gives us, along with the teaching of the Synoptics, that peculiar teaching respecting the pre-existent Divine nature of Jesus which, as far as can be ascertained, was to be found only in the Fourth Gospel, and which is consequently called Johannean; and that, besides this, he refers to the history, and adopts the language, and urges the arguments which are to be found only in St. John.

We have also shown that there are no internal considerations whatsoever for supposing that Justin did not make use of the Fourth Gospel. Instead, for instance, of the doctrine of St. John being a development of that held by Justin Martyr, the facts of the case all point to the contrary.

We must now see whether there is external evidence which makes it not only probable, but as certain as any fact in literary history can be, that Justin must have known and made use of our present Evangelists ; that if he was a teacher in such an acknowledged centre of ecclesiastical information or tradition as Rome, and *appears* to quote our Gospels (with no matter what minor variations and inaccuracies), he did actually quote the same and no other ; and if his inaccuracies, and discrepancies, and omissions of what we suppose he ought to have mentioned, were doubled or trebled, it would still be as certain as any fact of such a nature can be, that he quoted the Four Evangelists, because they must have been read and commented on in his day and in his church as the Memoirs of the Apostles, which took their place by the side of the prophets of the Old Testament in the public instruction of the Church. In order to this I shall have to examine the external evidence for the Canon of the New Testament—so far, that is, as the Four Gospels are concerned.

In doing this I shall not take the usual method of tracing the evidence for the various books in question downwards from the Apostolic time—the reader will find this treated exhaustively in "Dr. Westcott on the Canon"—but I shall trace it upwards, beginning at a time at which there cannot be the smallest doubt that the New Testament was exactly the same as that which we now possess.

For this purpose I shall take the Ecclesiastical History of Eusebius as the starting-point. The reader is, of course, aware that he is the earliest ecclesiastical writer whose history has come down to us, the historians who wrote before his time being principally known to us through fragments preserved in his book. He was born of Christian parents about the year A.D. 270, and died about 340. He probably wrote his history about or before the year 325.

The reader, though he may not have read his history, will be aware, from the quotations from it in "Supernatural Religion," that Eusebius carefully investigated the history of the Canon of Scripture, and also the succession of ecclesiastical writers. His history is, in fact, to a great extent, a sketch of early Church literature. In dealing with the history of the Canon, he particularly notices whether a large number of writers have quoted certain books of Scripture, of whose acceptance by the whole Church doubts were entertained. This is important, as it shows that not only himself, but the Church, during the three ages whose history he has recorded, did not receive books of Scripture except upon what they deemed to be sufficient evidence, and that evidence was the reception of each book from Apostolic times by the whole Church. I will now give the testimony of Eusebius to the authenticity of the Four Gospels.

First of all he describes the origin of the Gospel of St. Mark in the following words :—

" So greatly, however, did the splendour of piety enlighten the minds of Peter's hearers, that it was not sufficient to hear but once, nor to receive the unwritten doctrine of the Gospel of God, but they persevered, in every variety of entreaties, to solicit Mark as the companion of Peter, and whose Gospel we have, that he should leave them a monument of the doctrine thus orally communicated, in writing. Nor did they cease with their solicitations until they had prevailed with the man, and thus become the means of that history which is called the Gospel according to Mark. They say also, that the Apostle (Peter), having ascertained what was done by the revelation of the Spirit, was delighted with the zealous ardour expressed by these men, and that the history obtained his authority for the purpose of being read in the Churches. This account is given by Clement in the Sixth Book of his Institutions, whose testimony also is corroborated by that of Papias, Bishop of Hierapolis." (Bk. ii. chap. xv. Crusé's translation.)

This is narrated as having taken place in the reign of Claudius, *i.e.*, between A.D. 41 and A.D. 54.

The next Gospel whose origin he describes is that of St. Luke, in the following words :—

"But Luke, who was born at Antioch, and by profession a physician, being for the most part connected with Paul, and familiarly acquainted with the rest of the Apostles, has left us two inspired books, the institutes of that spiritual healing art which he obtained from them. One of these is his Gospel, in which he testifies that he has recorded, ' as those who were from the beginning eye-witnesses and ministers of the word,' delivered to him, whom also, he says, he has in all things followed. The other is his Acts of the Apostles, which he composed, not from what he had heard from others, but from what he had seen himself. It is also said that Paul usually referred to his Gospel, whenever in his Epistles he spoke of some particular Gospel of his own, saying, ' according to my Gospel.'" (Bk. iii. ch. iv. Crusé's translation.)

Further on, he describes the publication of the First and Fourth Gospels, thus :—

" Of all the disciples, Matthew and John are the only ones that have left us recorded comments, and even they, tradition says, undertook it from necessity. Matthew also, having first proclaimed the Gospel in Hebrew, when on the point of going also to other nations, committed it to writing in his native tongue, and thus supplied the want of his presence to them by his writings. But after Mark and Luke had already published their Gospels they say that John, who, during all this time, was proclaiming the Gospel without writing, at length proceeded to write it on the following occasion. The three Gospels previously written had been distributed among all, and also handed to him; they say that he admitted them, giving his testimony to their truth; but that there was only wanting in the narrative the account of the things done by Christ among the first of His deeds, and at the commencement of the Gospel. And this was the truth. For it is evident that the other three Evangelists only wrote the deeds of our Lord for one year after the imprisonment of John the Baptist, and intimated this in the very beginning of their history. For after the fasting of forty days, and the consequent temptation, Matthew indeed specifies the time of his history in these words, 'But, hearing that John was delivered up, he returned from Judea into Galilee.' Mark in like manner writes: 'But, after John was delivered up, Jesus came into Galilee.' And Luke, before he commenced the deeds of Jesus, in much the same way designates the time, saying, 'Herod thus added this wickedness above all he had committed, and that he shut up John in prison.' For these reasons the Apostle John, it is said, being entreated to undertake it, wrote the account of the time not recorded by the former Evangelists, and the deeds done by our Saviour, which they have passed by (for these were the events that occurred before the imprisonment of John), and this very fact is intimated by him when he says, 'This beginning of miracles Jesus made,' and then proceeds to make mention of the Baptist, in the midst of our Lord's deeds, as John was at that time 'baptizing at Ænon, near to Salim.' He plainly also shows this in the words, 'John was not yet cast into prison.' The Apostle, therefore, in his Gospel, gives the deeds of Jesus before the Baptist was cast into prison, but the other three Evangelists mention the circumstances after that event," &c. (Bk. iii. c. xxiv.)

The last extract which I shall give is from the next chapter, when he mentions " The sacred Scriptures which are acknowledged as genuine, and those that are not :"—

" This appears also to be the proper place to give a summary statement of the books of the New Testament already mentioned. And here among the first must be placed *the Holy Quaternion of the Gospels;* these are followed by the Book of the Acts of the Apostles; after this must be mentioned the Epistles of Paul, which are followed by the acknowledged First Epistle of John, also the First of Peter to be admitted in like manner. After these are to be placed, if proper, the Revelation of John, concerning which we shall offer the different opinions in due time. These, then, are acknowledged as genuine. Among the disputed books, although they are well known and approved by many, is reputed that called the Epistle of James and [that] of Jude. Also the Second Epistle of Peter, and those called the Second and Third of John, whether they are of the Evangelist, or of some other of the same name. Among the spurious must be numbered both the books called the Acts of Paul, and that called Pastor, and the Revelation of Peter. Besides these, the books called the Epistle of Barnabas, and what are called the Institutions of the Apostles. Moreover, as I said before, if it should appear right, the Revelation of John, which some, as before said, reject, but others rank among the genuine. But there are also some who number among these the Gospel according to the Hebrews, with which those of the Hebrews that have received Christ are particularly delighted." (Bk. iii. ch. xxv.)

Such are the statements of the oldest ecclesiastical historian whose work has come down to us.

With respect to the Gospels, he knows but four as canonical, and has never heard of any other as accepted by the Church. He mentions Apocryphal and disputed books. Amongst the latter he mentions the Gospel to the Hebrews as acceptable to a local church; but he is wholly ignorant of any doubt having ever been cast upon the authority of the four in any branch of the Catholic Church.

Now let the reader remember, that however Eusebius, like all other writers, might be liable to be mistaken through carelessness, or prejudice, or any other cause of inaccuracy; yet that each of these statements respecting the authorship of the various Gospels is, on all principles of common sense, worth all the conjectural criticisms of the German and other writers, so copiously cited in "Supernatural Religion," put together.

For, in the first place, Eusebius flourished about 1500 years nearer to the original source of the truth than these critics, and had come to man's estate within 200 years of the publication of the Fourth Gospel.

Now, at a time when tradition was far more relied upon, and so much more perfectly preserved and transmitted than in such an age of printed books and public journals as the present, this alone would make an enormous difference between a direct statement of Eusebius and the conjecture of a modern theorist. But far more than this, Eusebius had access to, and was well acquainted with, a vast mass of ecclesiastical literature which has altogether perished; and the greater part of which is only known to have existed through notices or extracts to be found in his work. For instance, in a few pages he gives accounts of writings which have perished of Papias (iii. c. 39), Quadratus and Aristides (iv. ch. 3), Hegesippus (iv. ch. 8 and 22), Tatian (iv. ch. 16), Dionysius of Corinth (iv. ch. 23), Pinytus (iv. ch. 23), Philip and Modestus (ch. 25), Melito (ch. 26), Apollinaris (ch. 27), Bardesanes (ch. 30).

These are all writers who flourished in the first three quarters of the second century, and I have only mentioned those whose writings, from the wording of his notices, Eusebius appears to have seen himself.

It is clear, I repeat, that the evidence of such an one on the authorship of the Gospels is worth all the conjectures and theories of modern critics of all classes put together.

We shall pass over very briefly the first sixty years of the third century, *i.e.* between A.D. 200 and the time of Eusebius. During these years flourished Cyprian, martyred A.D. 257; Hippolytus, martyred about A.D. 240; and Origen, died A.D. 254.

Respecting the latter, it appears from Eusebius that he published commentaries on the Gospels of St. Matthew and St. John. Of the latter Eusebius says the first five books were composed at Alexandria, but of the whole work on St. John only twenty-two books have come down to us. (Bk. vi. ch. 24.) Now Origen was born a few years (at the most twenty) after the death of Justin; and we have seen how the author of "Supernatural Religion" evidently considers the works of Justin to be anterior to the Fourth Gospel. Is it credible, or even conceivable, that a man of Origen's intellect, learning, and research should write twenty or thirty books of commentaries on a false Gospel which was forged shortly before his own time?

He expressly states that the Church knew of but four Gospels :—

" As I have understood from tradition respecting the four Gospels, which are the only undisputed ones in the whole Church of God throughout the world. The first is written according to Matthew, the same that was once a publican, but afterwards an Apostle of Jesus Christ, who, having published it for the Jewish converts, wrote it in Hebrew. The second is according to Mark, who composed it as Peter explained to him, whom he [Peter] also acknowledged as his son in his general epistle, saying, ' The elect Church in Babylon salutes you, as also Mark, my son.' And the third according to Luke, the Gospel commended by Paul, which was written 'for the converts from the Gentiles ; and, last of all, the Gospel according to John." Extract from Origen's first book of his commentaries on St. Matthew, quoted by Eusebius (vi. 25.)

As regards Cyprian, the following quotation will suffice :—

" The Church, setting forth the likeness of Paradise, includes within her walls fruit-bearing trees, whereof that which does not bring forth good fruit is cut off and is cast into the fire. These trees she waters with four rivers, that is, with the four Gospels, wherewith, by a celestial inundation, she bestows the grace of saving baptism." Cyprian, Letter lxxii. to Jubaianus.

As regards Hippolytus I have counted above fifty references to St. Matthew and forty to St. John, in his work on the " Refutation of Heresies," and " Fragments." I append in a note a passage taken from his comment on the Second Psalm, preserved to us by Theodoret. The reader will be able to judge from it from what sources he derived his knowledge of Christ. I give it rather for its devotional spirit than its evidence for the four.[1]

---

[1] " When He came into the world He was manifested as God and man. And it is easy to perceive the man in Him when He hungers

We now come to the conclusion of the second century. Between the years 180 and 200 or 210 A.D., there flourished three writers of whom we possess somewhat voluminous remains. Irenæus, who was born about 140 at the latest, who was in youth the disciple of Polycarp, who was himself the disciple of St. John. Irenæus wrote his work against heresies about the year 180, a little after he had succeeded Pothinus as Bishop of Lyons, and was martyred at the beginning of the next century (202).

Clement of Alexandria, the date of whose birth or death is uncertain, flourished long before the end of the second century, for he became head of the catechetical school of Alexandria about the year 190.

Tertullian was born about 150, was converted to Christianity about 185, was admitted to the priesthood in 192, and adopted the opinions of Montanus about the end of the century.

---

and shows exhaustion, and is weary and athirst, and withdraws in fear, and is in prayer and in grief, and sleeps on a boat's pillow, and entreats the removal of the cup of suffering, and sweats in an agony, and is strengthened by an angel, and betrayed by a Judas, and mocked by Caiaphas, and set at nought by Herod, and scourged by Pilate, and derided by the soldiers, and nailed to the tree by the Jews, and with a cry commits His spirit to His Father, and drops His head and gives up the ghost, and has His side pierced by a spear, and is wrapped in linen and laid in a tomb, and is raised by the Father from the dead. And the Divine in Him, on the other hand, is equally manifest when He is worshipped by angels, and seen by shepherds, and waited for by Simeon, and testified of by Anna, and inquired after by wise men, and pointed out by a star, and at a marriage makes wine of water, and chides the sea when tossed by the violence of winds, and walks upon the deep, and makes one see who was blind from birth, and raises Lazarus when dead for four days, and works many wonders, and forgives sins, and grants power to His disciples."

I shall first of all give the testimony of these three writers to the universal reception of the Four Gospels by the Church, and consider to what time previous to their own day their testimony upon such a subject must, of necessity, reach.

First of all, Irenæus, in a well-known passage, asserts that—

"It is not possible that the Gospels can be either more or fewer in number than they are."

He then refers to the four zones of the earth, and the four principal winds, and remarks that, in accordance with this,

"He Who was manifest to men has given us the Gospel under four aspects, but bound together by one Spirit."

Then he refers to the four living creatures of the vision in the Revelation, and proceeds,—

"And, therefore, the Gospels are in accord with these things, among which Christ is seated. For that according to John relates His original effectual and glorious generation from the Father, thus declaring, 'In the beginning was the word,' &c. . . . But that according to Luke, taking up His priestly character, commences with Zacharias the priest offering sacrifice to God. For now was made ready the fatted calf, about to be immolated for the finding again of the younger son. Matthew again relates His generation as a man, saying, 'The Book of the generation of Jesus Christ, the Son of David, the Son of Abraham;' and also, 'The birth of Jesus Christ was on this wise.' This, then, is the Gospel of His humanity, for which reason it is, too, that the character of an humble and meek man is kept up through the whole Gospel. Mark, on the other hand, commences with a reference to the prophetical spirit coming down from on high to men, saying, 'The beginning of the Gospel of Jesus

Christ, as it is written in Esaias the prophet,' pointing to the winged aspect of tho Gospel: and on this account he made a compendious and cursory narrative, for such is the pro. phetical character." (Iren., Bk. iii. ch. xi.)

Clement of Alexandria, speaking of a saying ascribed to our Lord, writes:—

"In the first place, then, in the four Gospels handed down amongst us, we have not this saying; but in that which is according to the Egyptians." (Miscellanies, iii. ch. xiii.)

Tertullian writes thus :—

"Of the Apostles, therefore, John and Matthew first instil faith into us; whilst, of Apostolic men, Luke and Mark renew it afterwards. These all start with the same principles of the faith, so far as relates to the one only God the Creator, and His Christ, how that He was born of the Virgin, and came to fulfil the law and the prophets. Never mind if there does occur some variation in the order of their narratives, provided that there be agreement in the essential matter of the faith in which there is disagreement with Marcion." (Tertullian against Marcion, iv. c. ii.)

Such are the explicit declarations of these three writers respecting the number and authorship of the Four. I shall give at the conclusion of this section some of the references to be found in these writers to the first two or three chapters in each Gospel.

It is but very little to say that they quote the Four as frequently, and with as firm a belief in their being the Scriptures of God, as any modern divine. They quote them far more copiously, and reproduce the history contained in them far more fully than any modern divine whom I have ever read, who is not writing specifically on the Life of our Lord, or on some part of His teaching contained in the Gospels.

But I have now to consider the question, "To what time, previous to their own day, or rather to the time at which they wrote, does their testimony to such a matter as the general reception of the Four Gospels of necessity reach back?"

Clement wrote in Alexandria, Tertullian in Rome or Africa, Irenæus in Gaul. They all flourished about A.D. 190. They all speak of the Gospels, not only as well known and received, but as being the only Gospels acknowledged and received by the Church. One of them uses very "uncritical" arguments to prove that the Gospels could only be four in number; but the very absurdity of his analogies is a witness to the universal tradition of his day. To what date before their time must this tradition reach, so that it must be relied upon as exhibiting the true state of things?

Now this tradition is not respecting a matter of opinion, but a matter of fact—the fact being no other than the reading of the Gospels or Memoirs of our Lord in the public service of the Church. The " Memoirs of our Lord," with other books, formed the Lectionary of the Church. So that every Christian, who attended the public assemblies for worship, must know whether he heard the Gospels read there or not.

Now any two men who lived successively to the age of sixty-five would be able to transmit irrefragable testimony, which would cover a hundred years, to the use of the Gospels in the lectionary of the Church.

During the last five years we have had a change in our Lectionary, which change only affects the rearrangement of the portions read each day out of the same Gospels, and every boy and girl of fifteen years old at the time would recognize the alteration when it took place. If it had occurred fifty years ago, any man or woman of sixty-five would perfectly remember the change. If it had occurred within the last hundred years, any person of sixty-five could bear testimony to the fact that, when he first began to be instructed in the nature of the Church Services, he was told by his elders that up to a time which they could perfectly recollect certain selections from Scripture had been read in Church, but that at such a period during their lifetime a change had been brought about after certain public debates, and that it received such or such opposition and was not at once universally adopted, which change was the reading in public of the present selection. It is clear then, that if all public documents were destroyed, yet any two men, who could scarcely be called old men, would be able to transmit with perfect certainty the record of any change in the public reading of Scripture during the last one hundred years.

But, supposing that instead of a change in the mere selections from the Gospels, the very Gospels themselves had been changed, could such a thing have occurred unnoticed, and the memory of it be so absolutely forgotten that neither history nor tradition preserved the smallest hint of it at the end of a short century?

Now this, and far more than this, is what the author of "Supernatural Religion" asks his readers to believe throughout his whole work.

We have seen how, before the end of this century, no other authoritative memoirs of Christ were known by the

Church, and these were known and recognized as so essential a part of the Christian system, that their very number as four, and only four, was supposed to be pre-figured from the very beginning of the world.

Now Justin lived till the year 165 in this century. He was martyred when Irenæus must have been twenty-five years old. Both Clement and Tertullian must have been born before his martyrdom, perhaps several years, and yet the author of " Supernatural Religion " would have us believe that the books of Christians which were accounted most sacred in the year 190, and used in that year as frequently, and with as firm a belief in their authenticity as they are by any Christians now, were un-used by Justin Martyr, and that one of the four was abso-lutely unknown to him—in all probability forged after his time.

We are persistently told all this, too, in spite of the fact that he reproduces the account of the Birth, Teaching, Death, and Resurrection of Christ exactly as they are contained in the Four, without a single additional cir-cumstance worth speaking of, making only such altera-tions as would be natural in the reproduction of such an account for those who were without the pale of the Church.

But even this is not the climax of the absurdity which we are told that, if we are reasonable persons, we must accept. It appears that the "Memoirs" which, we are told, Justin heard read every Sunday in the place of assembly in Rome or Ephesus which he frequented, was a Pales-tinian Gospel, which combined, in one narrative, the accounts of the Birth, Life, Death, and moral Teaching of Jesus, together with the peculiar doctrine and history

now only to be found in the Fourth Gospel. Conse_
quently this Gospel was not only far more valuable than
any one of our present Evangelists, but, we might almost
say, more worthy of preservation than all put together,
for it combined the teaching of the four, and no
doubt reconciled their seeming discrepancies, thus ob_
viating one of the greatest difficulties connected with
their authority and inspiration; a difficulty which, we
learn from history, was felt from the first. And yet,
within less than twenty years, this Gospel had been sup-
planted by four others so effectually that it was all but
forgotten at the end of the century, and is referred to by
the first ecclesiastical historian as one of many apocrypha
valued only by a local Church, and has now perished so
utterly that not one fragment of it can be proved to be
authentic.

But enough of this absurdity.

Taking with us the patent fact, that before the end of
the second century, and during the first half of the
third, the Four Gospels were accepted by the Church
generally, and quoted by every Christian writer as fully
as they are at this moment, can there be the shadow of a
doubt that when Justin wrote the account of our Lord's
Birth, which I have given in page 22, he had before
him the first and third Evangelists, and combined these
two accounts in one narrative? Whether he does this
consciously and of set purpose I leave to the author of
" Supernatural Religion," but combine the two accounts
he certainly does.

Again, when, in the accounts of the events preceding
our Lord's Death, Justin notices that Jesus commanded
the disciples to bring forth an ass and its foal (page 33),

can any reasonable man doubt but that he owed this to St. Matthew, in whose Gospel alone it appears?

Or when, in the extract I have given in page 20, he notices that our Lord called the sons of Zebedee Boanerges, can there be any reasonable doubt that he derived this from St. Mark, the only Evangelist who records it, whose Gospel (in accordance with universal tradition), he there designates as the "Memoirs of Peter?"

Or again, when, in the extract I have given in page 34, he records that our Lord in His Agony sweat great drops [of blood], can there be a doubt but that he made use of St. Luke, especially since he mentions two or three other matters connected with our Lord's Death, only to be found in St. Luke? Or, again, why should we assume the extreme improbability of a defunct Gospel to account for all the references to, and reminiscences of, St. John's Gospel, which I have given in Sections VIII. and IX. of this work?

So far for Justin Martyr.

We will now turn to references in three or four other writers.

In the Epistle of Vienne and Lyons we find the following:—

"And thus was fulfilled the saying of our Lord: 'The time shall come in which every one that killeth you shall think that he offereth a service to God.'"

This seems like a reference to John xvi. 2. The words, with some very slight variation, are to be found there and not to be found elsewhere. The letter of the Churches was written about A.D. 178 "at the earliest," we are told by the author of "Supernatural Religion."

Well, we will make him a present of a few years, and suppose that it was written ten or twelve years later, *i.e.* about A.D. 190. Now we find that Irenæus had written his great work, " Against Heresies," before this date. Surely, then, the notion of the writer of " Supernatural Religion," that we are to suppose that this was taken from some lost Apocryphal Gospel when Irenæus, Bishop of Lyons, had actually used a written Gospel which contains it, refutes itself.

We turn to Athenagoras.

We find in his work, " Plea (or Embassy) for the Christians " (ch. x.), the following :—

"But the Son of God is the Logos of the Father in idea and in operation, for after the pattern of Him and by Him were all things made, the Father and the Son being one [I and My Father are one], and the Son being in the Father, and the Father in the Son, in oneness and power of spirit," &c.   (John xiv. 10.)

Again (ch. xii.) :—

"Men who reckon the present life of very small worth indeed, and who are conducted to the future life by this one thing alone, that they know God and His Logos." [This is life eternal, that they may know Thee the only true God, and Jesus Christ whom Thou hast sent.]

Can the writer of " Supernatural Religion " be serious when he writes, " He nowhere identifies the Logos with Jesus ? "   Does the writer of " Supernatural Religion " seriously think that a Christian writer, living in 177, and presenting to the emperor a plea for Christians, would have any difficulty about identifying Jesus with that Son of God Whom he expressly states to be the Logos of God ?

The following also are seeming quotations from the Synoptics in Athenagoras.

" What, then, are those precepts in which we are instructed? 'I say unto you, love your enemies, bless them that curse, pray for them that persecute you, that ye may be sons of your Father which is in the heavens, who maketh his sun to rise on the evil and the good, and sendeth rain on the just and on the unjust.'

" ' For if ye love them which love you, and lend to them which lend to you, what reward shall ye have ? '

" ' For whosoever, He says, looketh on a woman to lust after her, hath committed adultery already in his heart.'

" ' For whosoever, says He, putteth away his wife and marrieth another, committeth adultery.' "

When we consider that in the time of Athenagoras, or very soon after, there were three authors living who spoke of the Gospels in the way we have shown, and quoted them in the way we shall now show, why assign these quotations to defunct Gospels of whose contents we are perfectly ignorant, when we have them substantially in Gospels which occupied the same place in the Church then as now ?

Note on Section XIX.

I HAVE asserted that the three authors, Tertullian, Clement of Alexandria, and Irenæus, all flourishing before the close of the second century, quote the four Gospels, if anything, more frequently than most modern Christian authors do. I append, in proof of this, some of the references in these authors to the first two or three chapters of our present Gospels.

IRENÆUS.

Matthew, i.

"And Matthew, too, recognizing one and the same Jesus Christ, exhibiting his generation as a man from the Virgin ····· says, 'The book of the generation of Jesus Christ the son of David, the son of Abraham.' Then, that he might free our mind from suspicion regarding Joseph, he says, 'But the birth of Christ was on this wise: when His mother was espoused,'" &c. (iii. xvi.)

Then he proceeds to quote and remark upon the whole of the remainder of the chapter.

"Matthew again relates His generation as a man." For remainder, see page 128.

"For Joseph is shown to be the son of Joachim and Jeconiah, as also Matthew sets forth in his pedigree." (iii. 21, 9.)

"Born Emmanuel of the Virgin. To this effect they testify that before Joseph had come together with Mary, while she therefore remained in virginity, she was found with child of the Holy Ghost." (iii. 21, 4.)

"Then again Matthew, when speaking of the angel, says, 'The angel of the Lord appeared to Joseph in sleep.' (iii. 9, 2.)

"The angel said to him in sleep, 'Fear not to take to thee Mary, thy wife'" (and proceeding with several other verses of the same chapter). (iv. 23, 1.)

Matthew, ii.

"But Matthew says that the Magi, coming from the East, exclaimed, 'For we have seen His star in the East, and are come to worship Him.'" (iii. 9, 2.)

"And that having been led by the star unto the house of Jacob to Emmanuel, they showed, by those gifts which they offered, who it was that was worshipped; myrrh, because it was He who should die and be buried for the human race; gold, because He was a king," &c., &c. (iii. 9, 2.)

" He, since He was Himself an infant, so arranging it that human infants should be martyrs, slain, according to the Scriptures, for the sake of Christ." (iii. 16, 4.)

Matthew, iii.

" For Matthew the apostle . . . . declares that John, when preparing the way for Christ, said to them who were boasting of their relationship according to the flesh, &c., ' O generation of vipers, who hath shown you to flee from . . . . . raise up children unto Abraham.' (iii. 9, 1.)

" As John the Baptist says, ' For God is able from these stones to raise up children unto Abraham.' " (iv. 7, 2.)

There are no less than six quotations or references to the ninth and tenth verses of this chapter, viz., iv. 24, 2; v. 34, 1; iv. 8, 3; iv. 36, 4; v. 17, 4.

" Now who this Lord is that brings such a day about, John the Baptist points out when he says of Christ, ' He shall baptize you with the Holy Ghost and with fire, having His fan in His hand,'" &c. (iv. 4, 3.)

" Having a fan in His hands, and cleansing His floor, and gathering the wheat,'" &c. (iv. 33, 1.)

" Who gathers the wheat into His barn, but will burn up the chaff with fire unquenchable." (iv. 33, 11.)

" Then, speaking of His baptism, Matthew says, ' The heavens were opened, and He saw the Spirit of God,'" &c. (iii. 9, 3.)

Mark, i.

" Wherefore Mark also says, ' The beginning of the Gospel of Jesus Christ the Son of God, as it is written in the prophets.' " (iii. 16, 3.)

" Yea, even the demons exclaimed, on beholding the Son, ' We know Thee who Thou art, the Holy One of God.' " (iv. 6, 6.)

Mark iv. 28.

" His Word, through whom the wood fructifies, and the fountains gush forth, and the earth gives ' first the blade, then the ear, then the full corn in the ear.'" (iv. 18, 4.)

Luke, i.

" Thus also does Luke, without respect of persons, deliver to us what he had learned from them, as he has himself testified, saying, ' Even as they delivered them unto us, who from the beginning were eye-witnesses and ministers of the Word.'" (iii. 14, 2.)

Another reference to same in preface to Book iv.

" Luke, also, the follower and disciple of the Apostles, referring to Zacharias and Elizabeth, from whom, according to promise, John was born, says, ' And they were both righteous before God, walking in all the commandments and ordinances of the Lord blameless,'" &c.   (iii. 10, 1.)

" And again, speaking of Zacharias, ' And it came to pass, that while he executed the priest's office,'" &c.   (*Ibid.*)

" And then, speaking of John, he (the angel) says : ' For he shall be great in the sight of the Lord,'" &c.   (*Ibid.*)

" In the spirit and power of Elias."   (iii. 10, 6.)

" Truly it was by Him of whom Gabriel was the angel who also announced the glad tidings of His birth · · · · in the spirit and power of Elias."   (iii. 11, 4.)

" But at that time the angel Gabriel was sent from God, who did also say to the Virgin, ' Fear not, Mary, for thou hast found favour with God.'"   (iii. 10, 2.)

" He shall be great, and shall be called the Son of the Highest," &c.   (iii. 10, 2.)

" And Mary, exulting because of this, cried out ; prophesy-ing on behalf of the Church, ' My soul doth magnify the Lord.'"   (iii. 10, 2.)

" And that the angel Gabriel said unto her, ' The Holy Ghost shall come upon thee,'" &c.   (iii. 21, 4.)

" In accordance with this design Mary the Virgin is found

obedient, saying, ' Behold the handmaid of the Lord, be it unto me according to Thy word.' " (iii. 22, 4.)

" As Elizabeth testified when filled with the Holy Ghost, saying to Mary, ' Blessed art thou among women,' " &c. (iii. 21, 5.)

" Wherefore the prophets . . . announced His Advent . . . in freeing us from the hands of all that hate us, that is, from every spirit of wickedness, and causing us to serve Him in holiness and righteousness all our days.' " (iv. 20, 4.)

Luke, ii.

" Wherefore Simeon also, one of his descendants, carried fully out the rejoicing of the patriarch, and said, ' Lord, now lettest Thou Thy servant,' " &c. (iv. 7, 1.)

" And the angel in like manner announced tidings of great joy to the shepherds who were keeping watch by night." (iv. 7, 1.)

" Wherefore he adds, ' The shepherds returned, glorifying and praising God for all which they had seen and heard.' " (iii. 10, 4.)

" And still further does Luke say in reference to the Lord, ' When the days of purification were accomplished they brought Him up to Jerusalem to present Him before the Lord.' " (iii. 10, 5.)

" They say also that Simeon, ' Who took Christ into his arms and gave thanks to God,' " &c. (i. 8, 4.)

" They assert also that by Anna, who is spoken of in the Gospel as a prophetess, and who after living seven years with her husband, passed all the rest of her life in widowhood till she saw the Saviour." (i. 8, 4.)

" The production, again, of the Duodecad of the Æons is indicated by the fact that the Lord was twelve years of age when He disputed with the teachers of the law," &c. (i. 3, 2.)

" Some passages, also, which occur in the Gospels receive from them a colouring of the same kind, as the answer which He gave His mother when He was twelve years old, ' Wist ye not that I must be about My Father's business ? ' " (i. 20, 2.)

Luke, iii.

" For because He knew that we should make a good use of our substance which we should possess by receiving it from another, He says, 'He that hath two coats let him impart to him that hath none, and he that hath meat let him do likewise.'" (iv. 30, 3.)

" For when He came to be baptized He had not yet completed His thirtieth year, but was beginning to be about thirty years of age; for thus Luke, who has mentioned His years, has expressed it." (ii. 22, 5.)

John, i.

" [John] thus commenced his teaching in the Gospel, 'In the beginning was the Word, and the Word was with God, and the Word was God,'" &c. (iii. 11, 1.)

" He (St. John) expresses himself thus: 'In the beginning was the Word,'" &c. (i. 8, 5.)

" Thus saith the Scripture, 'By the word of the Lord were the heavens made,' &c. And again, 'All things were made by Him, and without Him was nothing made that was made.'" (i. 22, 1.)

" For he styles Him 'A light which shineth in darkness, and which was not comprehended by it.'" (i. 8, 5.)

" And that we may not have to ask 'Of what God was the Word made flesh?' He does Himself previously teach us, saying, 'There was a man sent from God whose name was John. The same came as a witness that he might bear witness of that Light. He was not that Light, but that he might testify of the Light.'" (iii. 11, 4.)

" While the Gospel affirms plainly that by the Word, which was in the beginning with God, all things were made, which Word, he says, was made flesh and dwelt among us." (iii. 11, 2.)

To John i. 14, " The Word was made flesh," the references are absolutely innumerable. Those I have given already will suffice.

" For this is the knowledge of salvation which was wanting

to them, that of the Son of God, which John made known, saying, ' Behold the Lamb of God, who taketh away the sin of the world. This is He of whom I said, After me cometh a Man Who was made before me, because He was prior to me.' " (iii. 10, 2.)

" By whom also Nathaniel, being taught, recognized Him ; he to whom also the Lord bare witness that he was an Israelite indeed, in whom was no guile. The Israelite recognized his King, therefore did he cry out to Him, ' Rabbi, Thou art the Son of God. Thou art the King of Israel.' " (iii. 11, 6.)

John, ii.

" But that wine was better which the Word made from water, on the moment, and simply for the use of those who had been called to the marriage." (iii. 11, 5.)

" As also the Lord speaks in reference to Himself, ' Destroy this temple, and in three days I will raise it up.' He spake this, however, it is said, of the temple of His body." (v. 6, 2.)

CLEMENT OF ALEXANDRIA.

Matthew, i.

" And in the gospel according to Matthew the genealogy which begins with Abraham is continued down to Mary, the mother of the Lord. ' For,' it is said, ' from Abraham to David are fourteen generations, and from David to the carrying away into Babylon,' " &c. (Miscellanies, i. 21.)

Matthew, iii.

" For the fan is in the Lord's hand, by which the chaff due to the fire is separated from the wheat." (Instructor, i. 9.)

Matthew, iv.

" Therefore He Himself, urging them on to salvation, cries, ' The Kingdom of Heaven is at hand.' " (Exhortation to Heathen, ch. ix.)

Matthew, v.

" And because He brought all things to bear on the discipline of the soul, He said, 'Blessed are the meek, for they shall inherit the earth.'" (Miscellanies, iv. 6.)

Mark, i.

"For he also 'ate locusts and wild honey.'" [In St. Mat_thew the corresponding expression being 'His food was locusts and wild honey.'] (Instructor, ii. 11.)

Luke, iii.

"And to prove that this is true it is written in the Gospel by Luke as follows: 'And in the fifteenth year, in the reign of Tiberius Cæsar, the word of the Lord came to John, the son of Zacharias.' And again, 'Jesus was coming to His baptism, being about thirty years old,' and so on." (Miscellanies, i. 21.)

There are at least twenty more references to the accounts of the preaching of St. John in the third of St. Matthew, first of St. Mark, and third of St. Luke, in Clement's writings, which I have not given simply because it is difficult to assign the quotation to a particular Evangelist, as the account is substantially the same in the three.

Luke xii. 16-20.

"Of this man's field (the rich fool) the Lord, in the Gospel, says that it was fertile, and afterwards, when he wished to lay by his fruits and was about to build greater barns," &c. (Miscellanies, iii. 6.)

Luke xiii. 32.

"Thus also in reference to Herod, 'Go tell that fox, Behold, I cast out devils,'" &c. (Miscellanies, iv. 6.)

Luke xiv. 12, 13.

"He says accordingly, somewhere, 'When thou art called to a wedding recline not on the highest couch.' . . . . And elsewhere, 'When thou makest a dinner or a supper,' and again, 'But, when thou makest an entertainment, call the poor.'" (Instructor, ii. 1.)

" For it were not seemly that we, after the fashion of the rich man's son in the Gospel, should, as prodigals, abuse the Father's gifts." (Instructor, ii. ch. i.)

John, i.

" You have then God's promise; you have His love: become partakers of His grace. And do not suppose the song of salvation to be new, as a vessel or a house is new; for . . . . in the beginning was the Word, and the Word was with God, and the Word was God." (Exhortation to Heathen, ch. i.)

" For He has said, ' In the beginning the Word was in God, and the Word was God." (Instructor, viii.)

" Wherefore it (the law) was only temporary; but eternal grace and truth were by Jesus Christ. Mark the expressions of Scripture; of the law only is it said ' was given; ' but truth, being the grace of the Father, is the eternal work of the Word, and it is not said to *be given*, but *to be* by Jesus, *without whom nothing was*." (Instructor, i. 7.)

" The divine Instructor is trustworthy, adorned as He is with three of the fairest ornaments . . . . with authority of utterance, for He is God and Creator; for all things were made by Him, and without Him was not anything made: and with benevolence, for He alone gave Himself a sacrifice for us, ' For the Good Shepherd giveth His life for the sheep.' " (John x. 11.) (Instructor, i. 11.)

" For the darkness, it is said, comprehendeth it not." (Instructor, ii. 10.)

" Having through righteousness attained to adoption, and therefore ' have received power to become the sons of God.' " (Miscellanies, iv. 6.)

" For of the prophets it is said, ' We have all received of His fulness,' that is, of Christ's." (Miscellanies, i. 17.)

" And John the apostle says, ' No man hath seen God at any time. The only begotten God,' [oldest reading,] ' who is in the bosom of the Father, He hath declared Him.' " (Miscellanies, v. 12.)

John, iii.

"He that believeth not is, according to the utterance of the Saviour, condemned already." (Miscellanies, iv. 16.)

"Enslaved as you are to evil custom, and clinging to it voluntarily till your last breath, you are hurried to destruction; because light has come into the world, and men have loved the darkness rather than the light." (Exhortation to Heathen, 10.)

"'I must decrease,' said the prophet John." (Miscellanies, vi. 11.)

TERTULLIAN.

Matthew, i.

"There is, first of all, Matthew, that most faithful chronicler of the Gospel, because the companion of the Lord; for no other reason in the world than to show us clearly the fleshy original of Christ, he thus begins, 'The book of the generation of Jesus Christ, the son of David the son of Abraham.'" (On the Flesh of Christ, ch. xxii.)

"It is, however, a fortunate circumstance that Matthew also, when tracing down the Lord's descent from Abraham to Mary, says, 'Jacob begat Joseph, the husband of Mary, *of whom* was born Jesus.'" (On the Flesh of Christ, ch. xx.)

"You [the heretic] say that He was born *through* a virgin, not *of* a virgin, and *in* a womb, not *of* a womb; because the angel in the dream said to Joseph, 'That which is born in her is of the Holy Ghost.'" (*Ibid.* ch. xx.)

Matthew, ii.

"For they therefore offered to the then infant Lord that frankincense, and myrrh, and gold, to be, as it were, the close of worldly sacrifice and glory, which Christ was about to do away." (On Idolatry, ch. ix.)

Mark i. 4.

"For, in that John used to preach 'baptism *for* the remission of sins,' the declaration was made with reference to a future remission. (On Baptism, x.)

Mark i. 24.

" This accordingly the devils also acknowledge Him to be:
' We know Thee Who Thou art, the Son of God.' " (Against
Praxeas, ch. xxvi.)

Let the reader particularly remark this phrase. Tertullian quotes the last clauses differently from the reading
in our present copies, "The Holy One of God." -If
such a quotation had occurred in Justin, the author
of " Supernatural Religion " would have cited the phrase
as a quotation from a lost Gospel, and asserted that the
author had not even seen St. Mark.

Luke, i.

" Elias was nothing else than John, who came ' in the
power and spirit of Elias.' " (On Monogamy, ch. viii.)

" I recognize, too, the angel Gabriel as having been sent to
a virgin; but when he is blessing her, it is ' among women.' "
(On the Veiling of Virgins, ch. vi.)

" Will not the angel's announcement be subverted, that the
Virgin should ' conceive in her womb and bring forth a son ?'
. . . . . Therefore even Elizabeth must be silent, although
she is carrying in her womb the prophetic babe, which was
already conscious of his Lord, and is, moreover, filled with the
Holy Ghost. For without reason does she say, ' And whence
is this to me that the mother of my Lord should come to me?'
If it was not as her son, but only as a stranger, that Mary
carried Jesus in her womb, how is it she says, 'Blessed is
the fruit of thy womb ?' " (On the Flesh of Christ, ch. xxi.)

" Away, says he [he is now putting words into the mouth of
the heretic], with that eternal plaguy taxing of. Cæsar, and
the scanty inn, and the squalid swaddling clothes, and the
hard stable. We do not care a jot for that multitude of the
heavenly host which praised their Lord at night. Let the
shepherds take better care of their flock. . . . . Spare also
the babe from circumcision, that He may escape the pains

thereof; nor let Him be brought into the temple, lest He burden His parents with the expense of the offering; nor let Him be handed to Simeon, lest the old man be saddened at the point of death." (On the Flesh of Christ, ch. ii.)

"This He Himself, in those other gospels also, testifies Himself to have been from His very boyhood, saying, 'Wist ye not, says He, that I must be about my Father's business?'" (Against Praxeas, xxvi.)

John, i.

"In conclusion, I will apply the Gospel as a supplementary testimony to the Old Testament . . . . it is therein plainly revealed by Whom He made all things. 'In the beginning was the Word,'—that is, the same beginning, of course, in which God made the heaven and the earth—'and the Word was with God, and the Word was God,'" &c. (Against Hermogenes, ch. xx.)

I give only one reference to the first few verses, as the number in Tertullian's writings is enormous.

"It is written, 'To them that believed on Him, gave He power to be called Sons of God.'" (On Prayer, ch. ii.)

"But by saying 'made,' he [St. Paul] not only confirmed the statement 'the Word was made flesh,' but he also asserted the reality," &c. (On the Flesh of Christ, ch. xx.)

John, ii.

"[He Jesus] inaugurates in *water* the first rudimentary displays of His power, when invited to the nuptials." (On Baptism, ch. ix.)

The twenty-first chapter of the "Discourse against Praxeas" is filled with citations from St. John. I will give a small part.

"He declared what was in the bosom of the Father alone; the Father did not divulge the secrets of His own bosom. For this is preceded by another statement: 'No man hath seen

God at any time.' Then again, when He is designated by John as 'the Lamb of God.' . . . . This [divine relationship] Nathanael at once recognized in Him, even as Peter did on another occasion: 'Thou art the Son of God.' And He affirmed Himself that they were quite right in their convictions, for He answered Nathanael, 'Because I said I saw thee under the fig-tree, dost thou believe?' . . . . When He entered the temple He called it 'His Father's house,' [speaking] as the Son. In His address to Nicodemus He says, 'So God loved the world,' &c. . . . . Moreover, when John the Baptist was asked what he happened [to know] of Jesus, he said, 'The Father loveth the Son, and hath given all things into His Hands. He that believeth,' &c. Whom, indeed, did He reveal to the woman of Samaria? Was it not 'the Messias which is called Christ?' . . . He says, therefore, 'My meat is to do the will of Him that sent me, and to finish His work,'" &c. &c. (Against Praxeas, ch. xxi.)

THE EVIDENCE FOR MIRACLES.

I T does not come within the scope of this work to examine at any length the general subject of miracles.

The assertion that miracles, such as those recorded in
Scripture, are absolutely impossible, and so have never
taken place, must be met by the counter assertion that
they are possible, and have taken place. They are
possible to the Supreme Being, and have taken place by
His will or sufferance at certain perfectly historical
periods; especially during the first century after the
birth of Christ. When to this it is replied that miracles
are violations of natural law or order, and that it is
contrary to our highest idea of the Supreme Being to
suppose that He should alter the existing order of things,
we can only reply that it is in accordance with our
highest idea of Him that He should do so; and we say
that in making these assertions we are not unreasonable,
but speak in accordance with natural science, philosophy,
and history.

And, in order to prove this, we have only to draw
attention to the inaccuracy which underlies the use of
the term "law" by the author of "Supernatural Religion," and those who think as he does. The author

of " Supernatural Religion " strives to bring odium on the miracles of the Gospel by calling them " violations of law," and by asserting that it is a false conception of the Supreme Being to suppose that He should have made an Universe with such elements of disorder within it that it should require such things as the violation, or even suspension, of laws to restore it to order, and that our highest and truest idea of God is that of One Who never can even so much as make Himself known except through the action of the immutable laws by which this visible state of things is governed.

Now what is a law ?　The laws with which in this discussion we are given to understand we have to do, are strictly speaking limitations—the limitations of forces or powers which, in conception at least, must themselves be prior to the limitations.

Take the most universal of all so-called "laws," the law of gravitation.　The law of gravitation is the limitation imposed upon that mysterious force which appears to reside in all matter, that it should attract all other matter.　This power of attraction is called gravitation ; but instead of acting at random, as it were, it acts according to certain well-known rules which only are properly the " laws " of gravitation..

Now the very existence of our world depends upon the force of attraction being counteracted.　If, from a certain moment, gravitation were to become the only force in the solar system, the earth would fall upon the surface of the sun, and be annihilated ; but the earth continues in existence because of the action of another force—the projectile force—which so far counteracts the force of the sun's attraction, that the earth revolves round the sun instead of falling upon its surface. In this case the *law* of gravitation is not violated, or even suspended, but the force of gravitation is counteracted or modified by another force,

Again, the blood circulates through our bodies by means of another power or force counteracting the force of gravitation, and this is the vital power or force.

But why do we lift up our feet from the ground to go about some daily duty? Here comes another force—the force of will, which directs the action of some of the vital forces, but not that of others.

But, again, two courses of action are open to us, and we deliberately choose the one because we think that it is our duty, though it may entail danger or pain, or even death. Here is a still deeper force or power, the force of conscience—the moral power which is clearly the highest power within us, for it governs the very will, and sits in judgment upon the whole man, and acquits or condemns him according to its rule of right and wrong.

Here, then, are several gradations of power or force —any one of them as real as the others; each one making itself felt by counteracting and modifying the action of the one below it.

Now the question arises, is there any power or force clearly above the highest controlling power within us, *i.e.* above our conscience? We say that there is. There are some who on this point can reverently take up the words of our Great Master, "We speak that we do know." We believe, as firmly as we believe in our own existence, that this our conscience—the highest power within us—has been itself acted upon by a Higher Power still, a moral and spiritual Power, which has enlightened it, purified it, strengthened it, in fact renewed it.

Now, this purifying or enlightening of our moral powers has one remarkable effect. It makes those who have been acted upon by it to look up out of this present state of things for a more direct revelation of the character and designs of the Supreme Being. Minds who have experienced this action of a Superior Power upon them cannot possibly look upon the Supreme Being as revealing Himself merely by the laws of gravitation, or electricity, or natural selection. We look for, we desire a further and fuller Revelation of God, even though the Revelation may condemn us. We cannot rest without it. It is intolerable to those who have a sense of justice, for instance, to think that, whilst led by their sense of what is good and right, men execute imperfect justice, there is, after all, no Supreme Moral Governor Who will render to each individual in another life that just retribution which is assuredly not accorded to all in this life.[1]

Now this, I say, makes us desire a revelation of the Supreme Moral Governor which is assuredly not to be

---

[1] History affords multitudes of instances, but an example may be selected from one of the most critical periods of modern history. Let it be granted that Louis the Sixteenth of France and his Queen had all the defects attributed to them by the most hostile of serious historians ; let all the excuses possible be made for his predecessor, Louis the Fifteenth, and also for Madame de Pompadour, can it be pretended that there are grounds for affirming that the vices of the two former so far exceeded those of the latter, that their respective fates were plainly and evidently just? That whilst the two former died in their beds, after a life of the most extreme luxury, the others merited to stand forth through coming time, as examples of the most appalling and calamitous tragedy. (Mivart's " Genesis of Species," ch. ix.)

found in the laws which control mere physical forces. As Dr. Newman has somewhere said, men believe what they wish to believe, and assuredly we desire to believe that there is a supreme Moral Governor, and that He has not left us wholly in the dark respecting such things as the laws and sanctions of His moral government. But has He really revealed these? We look back through the ages, and our eyes are arrested by the figure of One Who, according to the author of "Supernatural Religion," taught a "sublime religion." His teaching "carried morality to the sublimest point attained, or even attainable, by humanity. The influence of His Spiritual Religion has been rendered doubly great by the unparalleled purity and elevation of His own character. He presented the rare spectacle of a life, so far as we can estimate it, uniformly noble and consistent with His own lofty principles, so that the "imitation of Christ" has become almost the final word in the preaching of His Religion, and must continue to be one of the most powerful elements of its permanence." (Vol. ii. p. 487.)

It is quite clear from this testimony of an enemy to the Christian religion, as it appears in the Scriptures, that if the Supreme Moral Governor had desired to give to man a revelation of the principles and sanctions of His moral government, He could not have chosen a more fitting instrument. Such a character seems to have been made for the purpose. If He has not revealed God, no one has.

Now, who is this Man Whose figure stands thus prominent above His fellows?

We believe Him to be our Redeemer; but before He

redeemed, He laid down the necessity of Redemption by making known to men the true nature of sin and righteousness, and the most just and inevitable Judgment of God. He revealed to us that there is One above us Who is to the whole race, and to every individual of the race, what our consciences are to ourselves—a Judge pronouncing a perfect judgment, because He perfectly knows the character of each man, perfectly observes and remembers his conduct, and, moreover, will mete out to each one a just and perfect retribution.

But still, how are we to know that He has authority to reveal to us such a thing as that God will judge the race and each member of it by a just judgment? Natural laws reveal to us no such judgment. Nature teaches us that if we transgress certain natural laws we shall be punished. But it teaches no certain judgment either in this life or in any future life which will overtake the transgression of moral laws. A man may defraud, oppress, and seduce, and yet live a prosperous life, and die a quiet, painless death.

How, then, are we to know that Jesus of Nazareth had authority to reveal that God will set all this right in a future state, and that He Himself will be the direct Agent in bringing the rectification about? How are we to know that what He says is true respecting a matter of such deep concern to ourselves, and yet so utterly unknown to mere physical nature, and so out of the reach of its powers? What proof have we of His Revelation, or that it is a Revelation? The answer is, that as what He revealed is above mere physical nature, so He attested it by the exhibition of power above physical nature— the exhibition of the direct power of God. He used miracles for this purpose; more particularly He staked the truth of His whole message on the miracle of His own Resurrection.[1] The Resurrection was to be the assurance of the perfection of both His Redemption and His Judgment.

Now, against all this it is persistently alleged that even if He had the power He could not have performed miracles, because miracles are violations of law, and the Lawgiver cannot violate even mere physical laws; but this specious fallacy is refuted by the simple assertion that He introduced a new power or force to counteract or modify others, which counteraction or modification of forces is no more than what is taking place in every part of the world at every moment.

Before proceeding further we will illustrate the foregoing by testing some assertions of the author of "Supernatural Religion."

"Man," he asserts, "is as much under the influence of gravitation as a stone is" (vol. i. p. 40). Well, a marble statue is a stone. Can a marble statue, after it is thrown down, rise up again of itself, and stand upon its feet?

Again—

"The law of gravitation suffers no alteration, whether

---

[1] What sign showest Thou us? Destroy this temple, and in three days I will raise it up: but He spake of the temple of His Body. (John ii. 19-21.) An evil and adulterous generation seeketh after a sign, and there shall no sign be given to it but the sign of the Prophet Jonas, for as Jonas was three days and three nights in the whale's belly, so shall the Son of Man be three days and three nights in the heart of the earth. (Matt. xii. 39, 40.) God commandeth all men everywhere to repent, because He hath appointed a day on which He will judge the world in righteousness by that man whom He hath chosen, whereof He hath given assurance unto all men in that He raised Him from the dead. (Acts xvii. 30.)

it cause the fall of an apple or shape the orbit of a planet" (p. 40).

Of course the "law" suffers no alteration, but the force of gravitation suffers considerable modification if you catch the apple in your hand, or if the planet has an impulse given to it which compels it to career round the sun instead of falling upon his surface.

Again (page 40):—

"The harmonious action of physical laws, and their adaptability to an infinite variety of forms, constitutes the perfection of that code which produces the order of nature. The mere superiority of man over lower forms of organic and inorganic matter does not lift him above physical laws, and the analogy of every grade in nature forbids the presumption that higher forms may exist which are exempt from their control."

The number of fallacies in this short passage is remarkable. In the first place laws never act, *i.e.* of themselves. They have to be administered. Forces or powers act under the restraint of laws. I think I am right in saying that all physical *laws*, as distinguished from forces, are limitations of force. No man can conceive of a law acting by itself. There is no such thing, for instance, as a "Reign of Law." A power acts or, if you please, reigns, according to a law, but laws of themselves can do nothing.

Again, the author says, "The mere superiority of man over lower forms of organic and inorganic matter does not lift him above physical laws."

Yes, it does, partially at least, for it enables him, in his sphere, to control the very forces whose action is limited by laws. The superiority of man is shown in his control of the powers of nature, and making them obey his will. All such inventions as the steam engine or the electric telegraph lift man above certain physical laws, by enabling him to control the forces with which those laws have to do.

Again, he writes: "The analogy of every grade in nature forbids the presumption that higher forms may exist which are exempt from their control." On the contrary, we assert that the analogy of every grade in nature encourages the presumption that higher forms may exist which can control these forces of nature far more directly and perfectly than we can.

To proceed. In page 41 we read :—

"If in animated beings we have the solitary instance of an efficient cause acting among the forces of nature, and possessing the power of initiation, this efficient cause produces no disturbance of physical law."

I cite this place, in order to draw attention to what I suppose must have struck the careful reader, which is the application of the term "solitary instance" to the action of animated beings amongst the forces of nature. If there had been but one animated being in existence, such an epithet might not have been out of place; but when one considers that the world teems with such beings, and that by their every movement they modify or counteract, in their own case at least, the mightiest of all nature's forces, and that no inconsiderable portion of the earth's surface owes its conformation to their action, we are astonished at finding all this characterized as the *solitary instance* of an efficient cause. But by a sentence at the bottom of this page we are enlightened as to the real reason for so strange a view of the place of vital powers in the universe. In the eyes of those who persist in, as far as possible, ignoring all laws except physical laws, even to the extent of endeavouring to prove that moral forces themselves are but mere developed forms of physical ones, all manifestations of powers other than those of electricity, gravitation, magnetism, and so forth, are anomalous, and we have the very word "anomaly" applied to them. "The only anomaly," he writes, "is our ignorance of the nature of vital force.[1] But do we know much more of the physical?"

Men who thus concentrate their attention upon mere physical laws or phenomena, get to believe in no others. They are impatient of any things in the universe except what they can number, or measure, or weigh. They are in danger of regarding the Supreme Being Himself as an "anomaly." They certainly seem to do so, when they take every pains to show that the universe can get on perfectly well without His superintending presence and control.

Whatever odium, then, may be attached to the violation of a natural *law*, cannot be attached to the action of a superior *force*, making itself felt amongst lower grades of natural forces.

If it be rejoined that this superior force must act

---

[1] This sentence seems extremely carelessly worded. The author cannot possibly mean that our ignorance is the anomaly, for throughout his whole work he assumes that ignorance is the rule in all matters, moral, physical, historical. The Fathers of the second century knew nothing of the Evangelists. St. John knows nothing of the writings of his brother Evangelists. They are all assumed to be ignorant of what they have not actually recorded. We know nothing of vital force, or physical force, or of a revelation. In fact, God Himself is the Unknowable.

according to law, we answer, certainly, but according to what law? Not, of course, according to the law of the force which it counteracts, but according to the law under which itself acts.

The question of miracles, then, is a matter of evidence; but we all know what a power human beings have of accepting or rejecting evidence according as they look for it or are prejudiced against it.

If men concentrate their thought upon the lower forces of the universe, and explain the functions of life, and even such powers as affection, will, reason, and conscience, as if they were modifications of mere physical powers, and ignore a higher Will, and an all-controlling Mind, and a personal superintending Providence, what wonder if they are indisposed to receive any such direct manifestation of God as the Resurrection of Jesus, for the Resurrection of Jesus is the pledge of a righteous Judgment and Retribution which, however it takes place, will be the most astounding " anomaly " amidst the mere physical phenomena of the universe, whilst it will be the necessary completion of its moral order.

The proof of miracles is then, as I said, a matter of evidence. When Hume asserts that "a miracle is a violation of the laws of nature," we meet him with the counter-assertion that it is rather the new manifestation in this order of things of the oldest of powers, that which originally introduced life into a lifeless world.

When he says that "a firm and unalterable experience has established these laws," we say that science teaches us that there must have been epochs in the history of the world when new forces made their appearance on the scene, for it teaches us that the world was once incandescent, and so incapable of supporting any conceivable form of animal life, but that at a certain geological period life made its appearance.

Now, we believe that it is just as wonderful, and contrary to the experience of a lifeless world, that life should appear on that world, as that it is contrary to the experience of the present state of things, that a dead body should be raised.

When he asserts that a miraculous event is contrary to uniform experience, we can only reply that it is not contrary to the experience of the Evangelists, of St. Peter and St. Paul, and of the other Apostles and companions of the Lord ; that it was not contrary to the experience of the multitudes who were miraculously fed, and of the multitudes who were miraculously healed. When it is replied to this, that we have insufficient evidence of the fact that these persons witnessed miracles, we rejoin that there is far greater evidence, both in quality and amount, for these miracles, especially for the crowning one, than there is for any fact of profane history ; but, if there was twice the evidence that there is, its reception must depend upon the state of mind of the recipient himself.

If a man, whilst professing to believe in " a God under whose beneficent government we know that all that is consistent with wise and omnipotent law is prospered and brought to perfection," yet has got himself to believe that such a God cannot introduce into any part of the universe a new power or force, as for instance that He is bound not to introduce vital force into a lifeless world, or mental power into a reasonless world, or moral power into a world of free agents, but must leave these forces to work themselves out of non-existence;—if a man, I say, has got himself to believe in such a Being, he will not, of course, believe in any testimony to miracles as accrediting a Revelation from Him, and so he will do his best to get rid of them after the fashion in which we have seen the author of "Supernatural Religion" attempt to get rid of the testimony of Justin Martyr to the use of the Four Gospels in his day.

I WILL now briefly dispose of two or three of the collateral objections against miracles.

1. The author of " Supernatural Religion " makes much of the fact that the Scripture writers recognize that there may be, and have been, Satanic as well as Divine Miracles, and he argues that this destroys all the evidential value of a miracle. He writes :—

" Even taking the representation of miracles, therefore, which Divines themselves give, they are utterly incompetent to perform their contemplated functions. If they are super-human, they are not super-Satanic, and there is no sense in which they can be considered miraculously evidential of any-thing." (Vol. i. p. 25.)

Now, this difficulty is the merest theoretical one,—a difficulty, as the saying is, on paper; and never can be a practical one to any sincere believer in the holiness of God and the reality of goodness. Take the miracle of miracles, the seal of all that is supernatural in our re-ligion, the Resurrection of Christ. If there be a con-flict now going on between God and Satan, can there be a doubt as to the side to which this miracle is to be assigned? It is given to prove the reality of a Redemp-tion which all those who accept it know to be a Redemption from the power of Satan. It is given to confirm the sanctions of morality by the assurance of a judgment to come. If Satan had performed it, he would have been simply casting out himself. If this miracle of the Resurrection be granted, all else goes along with it, and the children of God are fortified against the influence, real or counterfeit, of any diabolical miracle whatsoever.

The miracles of the New Testament are not performed, as far as I can remember, in any single instance, to prove the truth of any one view of doctrinal Christianity as against another, but to evidence the reality of the Mission of the Divine Founder as the Son of God, and " the Son of God was manifested that He might destroy the works of the devil."

2. With respect to what are called ecclesiastical miracles, *i. e.* miracles performed after the Apostolic age, the author of " Supernatural Religion " recounts the notices of a considerable number, assumes that they are all false, and uses this assumed falsehood as a means of bringing odium on the accounts of the miracles of Christ.

More particularly he draws attention to certain miracles recorded in the works of St. Augustine, of one at least of which he (Augustine) declares he was an eye-witness.

Now, the difficulty raised upon these and similar accounts appears to me to be as purely theoretical as the one respecting Satanic miracles. If there be truth in the New Testament, it is evident that the Founder of Christianity not only worked miracles Himself, but gave power to His followers to do the same. When was this power of performing miracles withdrawn from the Church ? Our Lord, when He gave the power, gave no intimation that it would ever be withdrawn, rather the contrary.

However, even in Apostolic times, the performance of them seems to have become less frequent as the Church became a recognized power in the world. For instance, in the earlier Epistles of St. Paul the exercise of miraculous gifts seems to have been a recognized part of the Church's system, and in the later ones (1 and 2 Timothy and Titus) they are scarcely noticed.[1] If we are to place any credence whatsoever in ecclesiastical history, the performance of miracles seems never to have ceased, though in later times very rare in comparison with what they must have been in the first age.

Now, if the miracles recorded by Augustine, or any of them, were true and real, the only inference is that the action of miraculous power continued in the Church to a far later date than some modern writers allow. If, on the contrary, they are false, then they take their place among hosts of other counterfeits of what is good and true. They no more go to prove the non-existence of the real miracles which they caricature, than any other counterfeit proves the non-existence of the thing of which it is the counterfeit. Nay, rather, the very fact that they are counterfeits proves the existence of that of which they are counterfeits. The Ecclesiastical miracles are clearly not independent miracles; true or false, they depend upon the miraculous powers of the early Church. If any of them are true, then these powers continued in the Church to a late date; if they are false accounts (whether wilfully or through mistake, makes no dif-

---

[1] Perhaps 1 Tim. i. 20, iv. 14; 2 Tim i. 6, may refer to such gifts; but the contrast between such slight intimations and the full recognition in 1 Cor. xii. and xiv. is very great.

ference), their falsehood is one testimony out of many to the miraculous origin of the dispensation.

Those recorded by Augustine are in no sense evidential. Nothing came of them except the relief, real or supposed, granted to the sufferers. No message from God was supposed to be accredited by them. No attempt was made to spread the knowledge of them; indeed, so far from this, in one case at least, Augustine is "indignant at the apathy of the friends of one who had been miraculously cured of a cancer, that they allowed so great a miracle to be so little known." (Vol. ii. p. 171.) In every conceivable respect they stand in the greatest contrast to the Resurrection of Christ.

Each case of an Ecclesiastical miracle must be examined (if one cares to do so) apart, on its own merits. I can firmly believe in the reality of some, whilst the greater part are doubtful, and many are wicked impostures. These last, of course, give occasion to the enemy to disparage the whole system of which they are assumed to be a part, but they tell against Christianity only in the same sense in which all tolerated falsehood or evil in the Church obscures its witness to those eternal truths of which it is " the pillar and the ground."

Now, all this is equally applicable to Superstition generally in relation to the supernatural. As the counterfeit miracles of the later ages witness that there must have been true ones to account for the very existence of the counterfeit, so the universal existence of Superstition witnesses to the reality of those supernatural interpositions of which it is the distorted image. If Hume's doctrine be true, that a miracle, *i.e.* a supernatural interposition, is contrary to universal experience and so incredible—if from the first beginning of things there has been one continuous sequence of natural cause and effect, unbroken by the interposition of any superior power, how is it that mankind have ever formed a conception of a supernatural power? And yet the conception, in the shape of superstition at least, is absolutely universal. Tribes who have no idea of the existence of God, use charms and incantations to propitiate unseen powers.

Now, the distortion witnesses to the reality of that of which it is the distortion ; the caricature to the existence of the feature caricatured. And so the universality of the existence of Superstition witnesses to the reality of these supernatural revelations and interpositions to which alone such a thing can be referred as its origin.

JEWISH CREDULITY.

ANOTHER argument which the author of " Super-natural Religion" uses to discredit miracles, is the superstition of the Jews, especially in our Lord's time, and their readiness to believe any miraculous story. He seems to suppose that this superstition reached its extreme point in the age in which Christ lived, which he calls "the age of miracles." He also assumes that it was an age of strong religious feeling and excitement. He says :—

" During the whole life of Christ, and the early propagation of the religion, it must be borne in mind that they took place in an age, and among a people, which superstition had made so familiar with what were supposed to be preternatural events, that wonders awakened no emotion, or were speedily superseded by some new demand on the ever ready belief." (Vol. i. p. 98.)

He proceeds to devote above twenty pages to instances of the superstition and credulity of the Jews about the time of Christ. The contents of these pages would be amusing if they did not reveal such deep mental degradation in a race which Christians regard as sacred, because of God's dealings with their fathers.

Most readers, however, of these pages on the Demonology and Angelology of the Jews will, I think, be affected by them in a totally different way, and will draw a very different inference, from what the writer intends. The thoughtful reader will ask, "How could the Evangelical narratives be the outcome of such a hotbed of superstition as the author describes that time to have been?" It is quite impossible, it is incredible that the same natural cause, *i. e.* the prevalence of superstition, should have produced about the same time the Book of Enoch and the Gospel according to St. Matthew. And this is the more remarkable from the fact that the Gospels are in no sense more Sadducean than the Book of Enoch. The being and agency of good and evil spirits is as fully recognized in the inspired writings as in the Apocryphal, but with what a difference! I append in a note a part of the author's reproduction of the Book of Enoch, that the reader may see how necessary it is, on all principles of common sense, to look for some very different explanation of the origin of the Evangelical narratives than that given by the author of "Supernatural Religion." [1]

---

[1] "The author [of the book of Enoch] not only relates the fall of the angels through love for the daughters of men, but gives the names of twenty-one of them, and their leaders, of whom Jequn was he who seduced the Holy Angels, and Ashbeel it was who gave them evil counsel and corrupted them. A third, Gadreel, was he who seduced Eve. He also taught to the children of men the use and manufacture of all murderous weapons, of coats of mail, shields, swords, and of all the implements of war. Another evil angel, named Penemue, taught them many mysteries of wisdom. He instructed men in the art of writing with paper and ink, by means of which, the author remarks, many fall into sin, even to the present day. Kaodejâ, another evil angel, taught the human race all the wicked practices of spirits and demons, and also magic and exorcism. The offspring of the fallen angels and of the daughters of men, were giants

In the Evangelical narratives I need hardly say the angels are simply messengers, as their name imports, and absolutely nothing more. When one describes himself it is in the words, " I am Gabriel that stand in the presence of God, and am sent to speak unto thee and to show thee these glad tidings."

On the credulity of the Jews in our Lord's time, I repeat the author's remarks :—

" During the whole life of Christ, and the early propagation of the religion, it must be borne in mind that they took place in an age, and among a people, which superstition had made so familiar with what were supposed to be preternatural events, that wonders awakened no emotion, or were speedily

---

whose height was 3,000 ells, of these are the demons working evil upon earth. Azayel taught men various arts, the making of bracelets and ornaments, the use of cosmetics, the way to beautify the eyebrows, precious stones and all dye-stuffs and metals, &c. The stars are represented as animated beings. Enoch sees seven stars bound together in space like great mountains, and flaming with fire, and he enquires of the angel who leads him on account of what sin they are so bound. Uriel informs him that they are stars which have transgressed the commands of the Most High, and they are thus bound until ten thousand worlds, the number of the days of their transgression, shall be accomplished." So far for the " Angelology." As to the demons, " Their number is infinite · · · · they are about as close as the earth thrown up out of a newly made grave. It is stated that each man has 10,000 demons at his right hand, and 1,000 on his left. The crush in the synagogue on the Sabbath arises from them, also the dresses of the Rabbins become so old and torn through their rubbing ; in like manner also they cause the tottering of the feet. He who wishes to discover these spirits must take sifted ashes and strew them about his bed, and in the morning he will perceive their footprints upon them like a cock's tread. If any one wish to see them, he must take the after-birth of a black cat, which has been littered by a first-born black cat, and whose mother was also a first-birth, burn and reduce it to powder, and put some of it on his eyes, and he will see them." (Vol. i. pp. 104 and 111). And this is the stuff which the author would have us believe was the real origin of the supernatural in the life of Jesus !

superseded by some new demand on the ever-ready belief." (Vol. i. p. 98.)

Now, if the records of our Lord's life in the Gospels are not a tissue of falsehoods from beginning to end, this account of things is absolutely untrue. The miracles of Jesus awakened the greatest astonishment, betokening a time as unfamiliar with the actual performance of such things as our own.

For instance, after the first casting out of a devil recorded in St. Mark, it is said :—

"They were all amazed, insomuch that they questioned among themselves, saying, What thing is this ? What new doctrine is this ? For with authority commandeth He even the unclean spirits, and they do obey Him." (Mark i. 29.)

In the next chapter, after the account of the healing of the sick of the palsy, it is said :—

"They were all amazed and glorified God, saying, We never saw it on this fashion." (ii. 12.)

Again (St. Luke v. 26), after the casting out of a devil: "They were all amazed." Again, Luke ix. 43 (also after the casting out of a devil), " They were all amazed at the mighty power of God."[1]

From the account in St. John, the miracle of the opening of the eyes of the man born blind seems to have excited unbounded astonishment:—

" Since the world began was it not heard that any man

---

[1] See also Mark v. 42 (healing of Jairus' daughter), " They were astonished with a great astonishment." Mark vii. 37 (healing of deaf man with impediment in his speech), " They were beyond measure astonished." Luke v. 9, " He was astonished at the draught of fishes ; " viii. 56, " Her parents were astonished."

opened the eyes of one that was born blind." "Can a devil open the eyes of the blind?" (John ix. 32, x. 21.)

But more than this. If there be any truth whatso-ever in the Gospel narrative, the disciples themselves, instead of exhibiting anything approaching to the cre-dulity with which the author of "Supernatural Re-ligion" taxes the contemporaries of Christ, exhibited rather a spirit of unbelief. If they had transmitted to us " cunningly devised fables," they never would have re-corded such instances of their own slowness of belief as is evinced by their conduct respecting the feeding of the four thousand following upon the feeding of the five thousand, when they ask the same question in the face of the same difficulty respecting the supply of food.

Above all, their slowness of belief in the Resurrection of Christ after their Master's direct assertion that He would rise again, is directly opposed to the idea sug-gested by the author of " Supernatural Religion," that they were ready to believe anything which seemed to favour His pretensions.

Now, it may be alleged that these instances of the slowness of belief on the part of our Lord's immediate followers, and the conduct of the multitudes who ex-pressed such wonder at His miracles, are contrary to one another, but they are not; for the astonishment of the multitudes did not arise from credulity in the least, but was the expression of that state of mind which must exist (no matter how carefully it is concealed), when some unlooked-for occurrence, totally inexplicable on any natural principles, presents itself. I cite it to show how utterly unfamiliar that age was with even the pretence of the exhibition of miraculous powers. If there be any substratum of truth whatsoever in the accounts of the slowness of belief on the part of the Apostles, it is a proof that our Lord's most familiar friends were anything but the superstitious persons which certain writers assume them to have been.

DEMONIACAL POSSESSION.

THE question of Demoniacal Possession now demands a passing notice.

The author of "Supernatural Religion" ascribes all such phenomena to imposture or delusion; and, inasmuch as these supposed miracles of casting out of evil spirits are associated with other miracles of Christ in the same narrative, he uses the odium with which this class of miracles is in this day regarded, for the purpose of discrediting the miracles of healing and the Resurrection of Jesus.

I cannot help expressing my surprise at the difficulty which some writers, who desire fully and faithfully to uphold the supernatural, seem to have respecting Demoniacal Possession. The difficulty seems to me to be not in the action of evil spirits in this or in that way, but in their existence. And yet the whole analogy of nature, and the state of man in this world, would lead us to believe, not only in the objective existence of a world of spirits, but in the separation of their characters into good and evil.

Those who deny the fact of an actually existing spiritual world of angels, if they are Atheists, must believe that man is the highest rational existence in the universe; but this is absurd, for the intellect of man is plainly very circumscribed, and he is slowly discovering laws which account for the phenomena which he sees, which laws were operative for ages before he discovered them, and imply infinitely more intellect in their invention, so to speak, and imposition and nice adjustment with one another, than he shows in their mere discovery. A student, for instance, has a problem put before him, say upon the adjustments of the forces of the heavenly bodies. The solution, if it evinces intelligence in him, must evince more and older intelligence in the man who sets him the problem; but if the conditions of the problem truly represent the acts of certain forces and their compensations, can we possibly deny that there is an intellect infinitely above ours who calculated beforehand their compensations and adjustments. All the laws of the universe must be assumed to be, even if they are not believed to be, the work of a personal intellect absolutely infinite, whose operations cannot be confined to this world, for it gives laws to all bodies, no matter how distant. The same reasoning, then, which shows that there is an intelligent will, because it can solve a problem, necessitates an infinitely higher Intelligence which can order the motions of distant worlds by laws of which our highest calculative processes are perhaps very clumsy representations.

Those who, like the author of "Supernatural Religion," are good enough to admit (with limitations) the existence of a Supreme Being, and yet deny the existence of a spiritual world above ours, seem to me to act still more absurdly. For the whole analogy of the world of nature would lead us to infer that, as there is a descending scale of animated beings below man reaching down to the lowest forms of life, so there is an ascending scale above him, between him and God. The deniers of the existence of such beings as angels undertake to assert that there are no beings between ourselves and the Supreme Being, because nature (meaning by nature certain lower brute forces, such as gravitation and elec. tricity), " knows nothing " of them.

The Scriptures, on the contrary, would lead us to believe that just as in the natural world there are grada. tions of beings between ourselves and the lowest forms of life, so in the spiritual world (and we belong to both worlds) there are gradations of beings between ourselves and God Who created all things.

The Scriptures would lead us to believe that these beings are intelligent free agents, and, as such, have had their time of probation—that some fell under their trial, and are now the enemies of God as wicked men are, and that others stood in the time of trial and continue the willing servants of God.

The Scriptures reveal that good angels act as good men do ; they endeavour, as far as lies in their power, to confirm others in goodness and in the service of God; and that evil angels act as evil men act, they endeavour to seduce others and to involve them in their own condemnation.

The Scriptures say nothing to satisfy our curiosity about these beings, as Apocryphal books do. They simply describe the one as sent on errands of mercy, and the other as delighting in tempting men and inflicting pain. The mystery of the fall of some of these angels, and their consequent opposition to God, is no difficulty in itself. It is simply the oldest form of that which is to those who believe in the reality of the holiness and goodness of God the great problem of the universe—the origin and continuance of evil. It is simply the counterpart amongst a world of free agents above us of what takes place according to the [so-called] natural order of things amongst ourselves.

That evil angels can tempt the souls of men, and in some cases injure their bodies, is not a whit more difficult than that evil men can do the same under the government of a God who exerts so universal a providence as is described in the Bible, and allowed to some extent by the author of " Supernatural Religion."

I confess that I cannot understand the difficulty which some Christian writers evidently feel respecting the existence of such a thing as Demoniacal *possession*, whilst they seem to feel, or at least they *express* no difficulty, respecting Demoniacal *temptation*. Demoniacal possession is the infliction of a physical evil for which the man is not accountable, but demoniacal temptation is an attempt to deprive a man of that for the keeping of which he is accountable, viz. his own innocence. Demoniacal possession is a temporal evil. The yielding to demoniacal temptation may cast a man for ever out of the favour of God. And yet demoniacal temptation is perfectly analogous to human temptation. A human seducer has it in his power, if his suggestions are received, to corrupt innocence, render life miserable, undermine faith in God and in Christ, and destroy the hopes of eternity—and a diabolical seducer can do no more.

Again, the Scriptures seem to teach us that these wicked spirits are the authors of certain temporal evils, and I do not see that there is anything unreasonable in the fact, if it be granted, that there are spirits who exist independent of bodily frames—that these spirits are free agents, and have different characters, and act according to their characters, and also that, according to the laws (*i.e.* within the limitations) of their nature, they have power to act upon those below them in the scale of being, just as we can act upon creatures below us according to the limitations, *i.e.* the laws, of our nature. We are in our way able to inflict evil or to ward off evil from our fellow creatures, under the limitations, or laws which a higher Power has set over us; and the Scriptures teach us that there are other beings in the great spiritual kingdom of God who are able to do us good or mischief under the conditions which the same Supreme Power has imposed on their action. So that the one thing which the Scriptures reveal to us is, that there is a far vaster spiritual kingdom of God than the human race.

With respect to demoniacal possession, our difficulties arise from two things—from our utter ignorance of the nature and real causes of mental diseases, and from our ignorance of the way in which purely spiritual beings can act upon beings such as ourselves, who ordinarily receive impressions only through our bodily organs. We know not, for instance, how God Himself acts upon our spirits, and yet, if He cannot, He has less power over us than we have over one another.

Respecting the fact of God permitting such a thing as possession, there is no more real difficulty than is involved in His permitting such a thing as madness. The symptoms of possession seem generally to have resembled mania, and ascribing certain sorts of mania to evil spirits is only assigning one cause rather than another to a disease of whose nature we are profoundly ignorant.[1]

Again, if we take into consideration the fact that in not a few cases madness is produced by moral causes, by yielding to certain temptations, as, for instance, to drunkenness, there will be still less difficulty in believing that madness, arising from the action of an evil being, may be the punishment of yielding to the seductions of that evil being.

The miraculous cure of demoniacal possession presents, I need hardly say, less physical difficulty than any other cure performed by our Lord. Assuming the presence of an evil spiritual existence in the possessed person coming face to face with the most exalted spiritual Power and Goodness, the natural result is that the one quails before the other.

But, in truth, all the difficulties respecting possession arise not so much from our ignorance, as from our dogmatism. We assert the dogma, or at least we quietly assume the dogma, that there are no spiritual or intellectual beings between ourselves and God ; or, if we shrink from an assertion which so nearly implies our own omniscience, we lay down that these superior beings, of whose laws we know nothing, can only act upon us in ways precisely similar to those on which we act upon one another.

---

[1] There cannot be the slightest doubt but that certain cases of madness or mania present all the appearances of possession as it is described in Scripture. Another personality, generally intensely evil, has possession of the mind, speaks instead of the afflicted person, throws the patient into convulsions,—in fact, exhibits all the symptoms of the ancient demoniacs. I have now before me the record of five or six such cases attested by German physicians.

SECTION XXIV.

COMPETENT WITNESSES.

ANOTHER objection which the author of " Super-natural Religion" urges against the credibility of our Lord's miracles, is that they were not performed before what he considers competent witnesses.

" Their occurrence [he writes] is limited to ages which were totally ignorant of physical laws." (Vol. i. p. 201.)

Again, he speaks of the age as one

" in which not only the grossest superstition and credulity prevailed, but in which there was such total ignorance of natural laws that men were incapable of judging of that reality [*i. e.* of miracles]." (P. 204.)

Again :—

" The discussion of miracles, then, is not one regarding miracles actually performed within our own knowledge, but merely regarding miracles said to have been performed eighteen hundred years ago, the reality of which was not verified at the time by any scientific examination." (P. 208.)

From this we gather that the author of " Supernatural Religion" considers that the miracles of Christ should have been tested by scientific men; but we ask, By what scientific men? It is clear that if the testing was to have been satisfactory to those who think like the author of " Supernatural Religion," they must have been scientific men who approached the whole matter in a spirit of scepticism.   Our Blessed Lord (I speak it with all reverence), if He cared to satisfy such men, should have delayed His coming to the present time, or should have called up out of the future, or created for this purpose, men who had doubts respecting the personality of God, who held Him to be fitly described as the Unknown and the Unknowable ; who, to say the least, were in a state of suspense as to whether, if there be a Supreme Being, He can reveal Himself or make His will known.   In fact, He must have called up, or created for the purpose, some individuals of a school of physicists which had no existence till 1,800 years after His time.   For, if He had called into existence such witnesses as Sir Isaac Newton, or Sir Humphrey Davy, or Cuvier, or Faraday, they would have fallen down and worshipped.

But, in truth, such witnesses, whether believing or sceptical, would have found no place for their science, for the miracles of Christ were of such a kind that the most scientific doubter could have no more accounted for them than the most ignorant.   The miracle of which, next to our Lord's own Resurrection, we have the fullest evidence, is that of the feeding of the 5,000 ; for it is recorded by each one of the four Evangelists.   Now, if this miracle had been performed in the presence of the members of all the scientific societies now in existence, their knowledge of natural laws could have contributed nothing to its detection or explanation.   They could have merely laid it down to trick or deception, just as any of the unscientific persons present could have done, and perhaps did.   The miracle was performed in the open. Our Lord must have been on some elevated ground where His voice could have reached some considerable part of the multitude, and on which every act of His could be observed. More than a thousand loaves would have been necessary, requiring the assistance of, say a hundred men, to collect them and bring them from a distance. This, too, is not one of those miracles which can be explained by the convenient hypothesis of a " substratum of truth." It is either a direct exhibition of the creative power of God, or a fiction as unworthy of a moment's serious consideration as a story in the "Arabian Nights."

It is folly to imagine that such an act required scientific men to verify it. If the matter was either a reality, or presented that appearance of reality which the narrative implies, then the scientific person would have been stupefied, or in trembling and astonishment he would have fallen on his face like another opponent of the truth ; or, may be, his very reason would have been shattered at the discovery that here before him was that very supernatural and divine Working in Whose existence he had been doing his best to persuade his fellow creatures to disbelieve.

The Scripture narratives, if they are not altogether devoid of truth, lead us to believe that our Lord performed His miracles in the face of three sects or parties of enemies, Pharisees, Sadducees, and Herodians; each one rejecting His claims on grounds of its own. They were also performed in a populous city, of which all the rulers and the mass of the inhabitants were hostile to His pretensions. Such a place could never have been chosen as the scene of a miraculous event, known by those who promulgated it to have had no foundation in truth, and withal assumed to have been known throughout the city at the time, and to have been productive of a series of results, miraculous and ordinary, which were asserted to have commenced at the moment of its occurrence.

The writer of " Supernatural Religion" would disparage the accounts of our Lord's supernatural works and Resurrection, because such accounts are to be found only in the writings of " enthusiastic followers," not in those of indifferent persons ; but the nature of the case almost excludes all other testimony : for the miracles of our Lord were wrought for an evidential purpose,—to convince the Jews especially that He was the Christ, the hope of their fathers, and, as such, was not only to be believed in, but to be obeyed and followed. The only sign of real true belief was that the man who professed to believe joined that society which was instituted for the purpose of propagating and keeping alive the truth of His Messiahship. If any one who professed to believe stopped short of joining this society, his testimony to miracles would have been valueless, for the miracles were wrought to convince him of the truth of a matter in which, if he believed, he was bound to profess his belief, and, if he did not, he laid himself open to the charge of not really believing the testimony.

Now, of course, the reader is aware that we have a signal proof of the validity of this argument in the well-known passage in Josephus which relates to our Lord. Josephus was the historian, and the only historian, of the period in which our Lord flourished. The eighteenth book of his " Antiquities of the Jews" covers the whole period of our Lord's life. If our Lord had merely attracted attention as a teacher of righteousness, which it is allowed on all hands that He did, it was likely that He would have been mentioned in this book along with others whose teaching produced far less results. Mention appears to be made of Him in the following words :—

" Now there was about this time Jesus, a wise man, if it be lawful to call him a man, for He was a doer of wonderful works, a teacher of such men as receive the truth with pleasure. He drew over to Him both many of the Jews and many of the Gentiles. He was [the] Christ. And when Pilate, at the suggestion of the principal men among us, had condemned Him to the cross, those that loved Him at the first did not forsake Him; for He appeared to them alive again the third day; as the Divine prophets had foretold these and ten thousand other wonderful things concerning Him. And the tribe of Christians, so named from Him, are not extinct at this day."

Now, on external grounds there seems little doubt of the genuineness of this passage. It is in all copies of the historian's work, and is quoted in full by Eusebius, though not alluded to by fathers previous to his day.[1] If it is an interpolation, it must have been by the hand of a Christian; and yet it is absolutely inconceivable that any Christian should have noticed the Christian Church in such words as " the tribe of Christians, so named from Him, are not extinct at this day." It would have been absurd beyond measure to have described the Christians, so early as Justin's time even, as

---

[1] The reader will find the references to it discussed in a dissertation at the end of Whiston's " Josephus." Lardner utterly denies its authenticity. Daubuz, however, has, I think, clearly proved its style and phraseology to be those of Josephus.

"not extinct," when they were filling the world with
their doctrine, and their increase was a source of great
perplexity and trouble to the Roman Government. It is
just what a Jew of Josephus' time would have written
who really believed that Jesus wrought miracles, but
expected that nothing permanent would result from
them.

And yet there can be no doubt but that the passage is
open to this insurmountable objection, that if Josephus
had written it he would have professed himself a Christian, or a man of incredible inconsistency. Setting aside
the difficulty connected with the acknowledgment of
Jesus as the Christ, inasmuch as this name was frequently
given to Him by those who did not believe in Him, yet
how could Josephus state that His Resurrection was
predicted by the prophets of his nation, and continue in
appearance an unbeliever ?

But, whether genuine or not, this passage is decisive
as to the impossibility of what is styled an independent
testimony to our Lord : " He that is not with Me is
against Me." The facts of our Lord's chief miracles and
Resurrection were such, that the nearer men lived to the
time the more impossible it would have been for them
to have suspended their judgment.

So that, instead of having the witness of men who, by
their prudent suspension of judgment, betrayed their
lurking unbelief, we have the testimony of men who, by
their surrender of themselves, soul and body, evinced
their undoubting faith in a matter in which there could
be really no middle opinion.

Section XXV.

DATE OF TESTIMONY.

ONE point remains—the time to which the testimony to our Lord's miracles reaches back. Can it be reasonably said to reach to within fifty years of His Death, or to within twenty, or even nearer?

The author of " Supernatural Religion" asserts that it was not contemporaneous or anything like it. In fact, one might infer from his book that the miracles of Christ were not heard of till say a century, or three quarters of a century, after His time, for he says, " they were never heard of out of Palestine until long after the events are said to have occurred." [1] (P. 192.)

In such a case, " long after" is very indefinite. It may be a century, or three quarters of a century, or perhaps half a century. It cannot be less, for every generation contains a considerable number of persons whose memories reach back for forty or fifty years. In a place of 3,000 inhabitants, in which I am now writing, there are above fifty persons who can perfectly remember

---

[1] Singular that he should say " out of Palestine," for if they were false they would be first heard of at a distance from the scene of their supposed occurrence. Jerusalem, so full of bitter enemies of Christ, was the last place in which His Resurrection was likely to be promulgated.

all that took place in 1830. There are some whose memories reach to twenty years earlier. Now let the reader try and imagine, if he can, the possibility of ascribing a number of remarkable acts—we will not say miraculous ones—to some one who died in 1830, and assuming also that these events were the basis of a society which had commenced with his death, and was now making way, and that the chief design of the society was to make known or keep up the memory of these events, and that there had been a literature written between the present time and the time of the said man's death, every line of which had been written on the assumption that the events in question were true, and yet these events had never really taken place. We must also suppose that the person upon whom these acts are attempted to be fastened was regarded with intense dislike by the great majority of his contemporaries, who did all they could to ruin him when alive, and blacken his memory after he had died, and who looked with especial dislike on the idea that he was supposed to have done the acts in question. Let the reader, I say, try and imagine all this, and he will see that, in the case of our Lord, the author's "long after" must be sixty or seventy years at the least; more likely a hundred.

Let us now summon another witness to the supernatural, whose testimony we promised to consider, and this shall be Clement of Rome—the earliest author to whom it has suited the purpose of the author of "Supernatural Religion" to refer.

If we are to rely upon the almost universal consent of ancient authors rather than the mere conjectures of modern critics, he is the person alluded to by St. Paul in the words, "With Clement also, and with other my fellow labourers, whose names are written in the book of life." (Phil. iv. 3.)

Of this man Eusebius writes:—

"In the twelfth year of the same reign (Domitian's), after Anencletus had been bishop of Rome twelve years, he was succeeded by Clement, whom the Apostle, in his Epistle to the Philippians, shows had been his fellow-labourer in these words: 'With Clement also and the rest of my fellow-labourers, whose names are in the book of life.' Of this Clement there is one Epistle extant, acknowledged as genuine, of considerable length and of great merit, which he wrote in the name of the Church at Rome, to that of Corinth, at the time when there was a dissension in the latter. This we know to have been publicly read for common benefit, in most of the Churches both in former times and in our own." (Eccles. Hist. B. III. xv. xvi.)

Origen confirms this. Clement of Alexandria reproduces several pages from his Epistle, calling him "The Apostle Clement,"[1] and Irenæus speaks of him as the companion of the Apostles:—

"This man, as he had seen the blessed Apostles and been conversant with them, might be said to have the preaching of the Apostles still echoing [in his ears], and their traditions before his eyes." (Bk. III. ch. iii. 3.)

Irenæus, it is to be remembered, died at the end of the second century, and his birth is placed within the first quarter of it, so that, in all probability, he had known numbers of Christians who had conversed with Clement.

According to the author of "Supernatural Religion,"

---

[1] Miscellanies, IV. ch. xvii.

the great mass of critics assign the Epistle of Clement to between the years A.D. 95-100.

In dealing with this Epistle I shall, for argument's sake, assume that Clement quoted from an earlier Gospel than any one of our present ones, and that the one he quoted might be the Gospel according to the Hebrews, and I shall ask the same question that I asked respecting Justin Martyr—What views of Christ's Person and work and doctrine did he derive from this Gospel of his ?

The Epistle of Clement is one in which we should scarcely expect to find much reference to the Supernatural, for it is written throughout for the one practical purpose of healing the divisions in the Church of Corinth. These the writer ascribes to envy, and cites a number of Scripture examples of the evil effects of this disposition and the good effects of the contrary one. He adheres to this purpose throughout, and every word he writes bears more or less directly on his subject. Yet in this document, from which, by its design, the subject of the supernatural seems excluded, we have all the leading features of supernatural Christianity. We have the Father sending the Son (ch. xlii.) ; we have the Son coming of the seed of Jacob according to the Flesh (ch. xxxii.); we have the words, "Our Lord Jesus Christ, the sceptre of the Majesty of God, did not come in the pomp of pride and arrogance, although He might have done so, but in a lowly condition, as the Holy Spirit had declared regarding Him" (ch. xvi.); and at the end of the same we have :—

" If the Lord thus humbled Himself, what shall we do who have through Him come under the yoke of His grace ? "

Clement describes Him in the words of the Epistle to the Hebrews as One—

"Who, being the brightness of His [God's] Majesty, is by so much greater than the angels as He hath by inheritance obtained a more excellent name than they." (Ch. xxxvi.)

We have Clement speaking continually of the Death of Jesus as taking place for the highest of supernatural purposes,—the reconciliation of all men to God. " Let us look," he writes, " steadfastly to the Blood of Christ, and see how precious that Blood is to God, which, having been shed for our salvation, has set the grace of repentance before the whole world." (Ch. vii.) Again, " And thus they made it manifest that Redemption should flow through the Blood of the Lord to all them that believe and hope in God." (Ch. xii.) Again, " On account of the love He bore us, Jesus Christ our Lord gave His Blood for us by the will of God, His Flesh for our flesh, and His Soul for our souls." (Ch. xlix.) His sufferings are apparently said by Clement to be the sufferings of God. (Ch. ii.) But, above all, the statement of the truth of our Lord's Resurrection, and of ours through His, is as explicit as possible :—

"Let us consider, beloved, how the Lord continually proves to us that there shall be a future resurrection, of which He has rendered the Lord Jesus the first fruits by raising Him from the dead." (Ch. xxiv.)
"[The Apostles] having therefore received their orders, and being fully assured by the Resurrection of our Lord Jesus Christ, and established in the Word of God, with full assurance of the Holy Ghost, they went forth proclaiming that the Kingdom of God was at hand." (Ch. xlii.)

When we look to Clement's theology, we find it to have been what would now be called, in the truest and best sense of the word, "Evangelical," thus :—

"We too, being called by His Will in Christ Jesus, are not justified by ourselves, nor by our own wisdom, or understanding, or godliness, or works which we have wrought in holiness of heart ; but by that faith through which from the beginning Almighty God has justified all men." (Ch. xxxii.)

Again :—

"All these the Great Creator and Lord of all has appointed to exist in peace and harmony ; while He does good to all, but most abundantly to us who have fled for refuge to His compassion through Jesus Christ our Lord."

And he ends his Epistle with the following prayer :—

"May God, who seeth all things, and Who is the Ruler of all Spirits and the Lord of all Flesh—Who chose our Lord Jesus, and us through Him to be a peculiar people—grant to every soul that calleth upon His glorious and holy Name, faith, fear, peace, patience, long suffering, self-control, purity and sobriety, to the well pleasing of His Name through our High Priest and Protector Jesus Christ." (Ch. lviii.)

But with all this his Christianity seems to have been Ecclesiastical, in the technical sense of the word. He seems to have had a much clearer and firmer hold than Justin had of the truth that Christ instituted, not merely a philosophy or system of teaching, but a mystical body or visible Church, having its gradations of officers corresponding to the officers of the Jewish Ecclesiastical system, and its orderly arrangements of worship. (Ch. xl-xlii.)

Now this is the Christianity of a man who lived at least sixty or seventy years nearer to the fountain head of Christian truth than did Justin Martyr, whose witness to dogmatical or supernatural Christianity we have shown at some length.

It is also gathered out of a comparatively short book, not one sixth of the length of the writings of Justin, and composed solely for an undogmatic purpose.

His views of Christ and His work are precisely the same as those of Justin. By all rule of rationalistic analogy they ought to have been less " ecclesiastical," but in some respects they are more so.

Clement certainly seems to bring out more fully our Lord's Resurrection (taking into consideration, that is, the scope of his one remaining book and its brevity), and the Resurrection of Christ is the crowning miracle which stamps the whole dispensation as supernatural.

So far, then, as the Supernatural is concerned, it makes no difference whatsoever whether Clement used the Gospel according to St. Matthew or the Gospel according to the Hebrews. His Gospel, whatever it was, not only filled his heart with an intense and absorbing love of Christ, and a desire that all men should imitate Him, but it filled his mind with that view of the religion of Christ which we call supernatural and evangelical, but which the author of " Supernatural Religion" calls ecclesiastical.

The question now arises, not so much from whom, but when, did he receive this view of Christ and His system. I do not mean, of course, the more minute features, but the substance. To what period must his reminiscences as a Christian extend? What time must his experiences cover? Irenæus, in the place I have quoted, speaks of him as the companion of Apostles, Clement of Alexandria as an Apostle, Eusebius and Origen as the fellow-labourer of St. Paul. Now, I will not at present insist upon the more than likelihood that such was the fact. I will, for argument's sake, assume that he was some other Clement; but, whoever he was, one thing respecting him is certain —that the knowledge of Christianity was not poured into him at the moment when he wrote his Epistle, nor did he receive it ten—twenty—thirty years before. St. Peter and St. Paul were martyred in A.D. 68; the rest of the Apostolic College were dispersed long before. This Epistle shows little or no trace of the peculiar Johannean teaching or tradition of the Apostle who survived all the others; so, unless he had received his Christian teaching some years before the Martyrdom of the two Apostles Peter and Paul, that is, some time before A.D. 68, probably many years, I do not see that there can have been the smallest ground even for the tradition of the very next generation after his own that he knew the Apostles. Such a tradition could not possibly have been connected with the name of a man who became a Christian late in the century.

Now, supposing that he was sixty-five years old when he wrote his Epistle, he was born about the time of our Lord's Death: he was consequently a contemporary of the generation that had witnessed the Death and Resurrection of Christ and the founding of the Church. If he had ever been in Jerusalem before its destruction, he must have fallen in with multitudes of surviving Christians of the 5,000 who were converted on and just after the day of Pentecost.

His Christian reminiscences, then, must have extended far into the age of the contemporaries of Christ. A man who was twenty-five years old at the time of the Resurrection of Christ would scarcely be reckoned an old man at the time of the destruction of Jerusalem. Clement consequently might have spent twenty of the best years of his life in the company of persons who were old enough to have seen the Lord in the Flesh.[1]

So that his knowledge of the Death and Resurrection of Christ, and the founding of the Church, even if he had never seen St. Paul or any other Apostle, must have been derived from a generation of men, all the older members of which were Christians of the Pentecostal period.

Now when we come to compare the Epistle of Clement with the only remaining Christian literature of the earliest period, *i. e.* the earlier Epistles of St. Paul, we find both the account of Christ and the Theology built upon that account, to be the same in the one and in the other.

The supernatural fact respecting Christ to which the earliest Epistles of St. Paul most prominently refer, was His Resurrection as the pledge of ours, and this is the fact respecting Christ which is put most prominently forward by Clement, and for the same purpose. The First Epistle to the Corinthians is referred to by Clement in the words:—

---

[1] Let the reader remember that, if this be an assumption, the contrary assumption is infinitely the more unlikely. Our assumption is founded on the direct assertion of two writers of the second century, one of whom asserts that Clement was a close companion of Apostles, another that he was an Apostle: meaning, of course, such an one as Barnabas. A writer of the early part of the next century, Origen, asserts that he was the person mentioned in St. Paul's Epistle, and the principal Ecclesiastical Historian who lived within two hundred years of his time corroborates this.

" Take up the Epistle of the Blessed Apostle Paul. What did he write to you at the time when the Gospel first began to be preached? Truly, under the inspiration of the Spirit ($\pi\nu\epsilon\upsilon\mu\alpha\tau\iota\kappa\hat{\omega}\varsigma$) he wrote to you concerning himself and Cephas and Apollos, because even then parties had been formed among you.". (Ch. xlvii.)

The other reproductions of the language of St. Paul's Epistles are numerous, and I give them in a note.[1] The reader will see at a glance that the Theology or Christ-

---

[1] " Ye .... were more willing to give than to receive " (ch. ii.). A reminiscence of St. Paul's quotation of Christ's words to be found in Acts xx. 35.

" Ready to every good work" (ch. ii.). Titus iii. 1. " Every kind of honour and happiness was bestowed upon you" (ch. iii.). Reminiscence of 1 Corinth. iv. 8.

" Let us be imitators of them who in goat skins and sheep skins went about proclaiming the coming of Christ " (ch. xvii). Heb. xi. 37.

" To us who have fled for refuge to his compassions" (ch. xx.). Reminiscence of Heb. vii.

" Let us esteem those who have the rule over us." 1 Thess. v. 12, 13; Heb. xiii. 17.

" Not by preferring one to another." 1 Tim. v. 21.

" A future Resurrection, of which He has rendered the Lord Jesus the first fruits by raising Him from the dead" (ch. xxiv.). 1 Cor. xv. 20; Col. i. 18.

" Nothing is impossible with God except to lie " (ch. xxvii.). Tit. i. 2; Heb. vi. 18.

" From whom [Jacob] was descended our Lord Jesus Christ according to the flesh" (ch. xxxii.). Rom. ix. 5.

" For [Scripture] saith, ' eye hath not seen,' " &c. (ch. xxxiv.). 1 Cor. ii. 9.

" Not only they that do them, but also those that take pleasure in them that do them" (ch. xxxv.). Rom. i. 32. Ch. xxxvi. contains distinct reference to Heb. i. I gave an extract above.

" Let us take our body for an example. The head is nothing without the feet .... yea, the very smallest members of our body are necessary and useful " (ch. xxxvii.), 1 Corinth. xii. 12, &c.

" Let every one be subject to his neighbour according to the special gift bestowed upon him" ($\kappa\alpha\theta\grave{\omega}\varsigma$ $\kappa\alpha\grave{\iota}$ $\grave{\epsilon}\tau\acute{\epsilon}\theta\eta$ $\grave{\epsilon}\nu$ $\tau\hat{\wp}$ $\chi\alpha\rho\acute{\iota}\sigma\mu\alpha\tau\iota$ $\alpha\grave{\upsilon}\tau o\hat{\upsilon}$) (ch. xxxviii.). Rom. xii. 1-4; Ephes. iv. 8-12.

ology of Clement was that of the earliest writings of the Church of which we have any remains, and to these he himself frequently and unmistakably refers.

The earlier Epistles of St. Paul, as those to the Thessalonians, Galatians, Corinthians, and Romans, are acknowledged on all hands, even by advanced German Rationalists, to be the genuine works of the Apostle Paul; indeed one might as well deny that such a man ever existed as question their authenticity. The First Epistle to the Corinthians, which is the longest and most dogmatic of the earlier ones, cannot have been written after the year 58. In a considerable number of chronological tables to which I have referred, the earliest date is the year 52, and the latest 58.

To the First Epistle to the Thessalonians, which is undoubtedly the earliest of all, the earliest date assigned is 47, and the latest 53.

Now it is ever to be remembered that in each of these —the First to the Thessalonians and the First to the Corinthians—we have enunciations of the great crowning supernatural event of Scripture—the Resurrection of Christ and our Resurrection as depending upon it, which are unsurpassed in the rest of Scripture.

So that in the first Christian writing which has come

"The blessed Moses, also, ' a faithful servant in all his house' " (ch. xliii.). Heb. iii. 5.

" Have we not all one God and one Christ? Is there not one Spirit of grace poured upon us? Have we not one calling in Christ?" (ch. xlvi.). Ephes. iv. 4-6.

" And have reached such a height of madness as to forget that we are members one of another" (ch. xlvi.). Rom. xii. 5.

" Love beareth all things . . . is long suffering in all things " (ch. xlix.). 1 Cor. xiii. 4.

down to us, we have the great fact of Supernatural Religion, which carries with it all the rest.

The fullest enunciation of the evidences of the Resurrection is in a writing whose date cannot be later than 58, and runs thus :—

" Moreover, brethren, I declare unto you the Gospel which I preached unto you, which also ye have received, and wherein ye stand; by which also ye are saved, if ye keep in memory what I preached unto you, unless ye have believed in vain. For I delivered unto you first of all that which I also received, how that Christ died for our sins according to the Scriptures ; and that He was buried, and that He rose again the third day according to the Scriptures. And that He was seen of Cephas, then of the twelve. After that [1] He was seen of above five hundred brethren at once, of whom the greater part remain unto this present [twenty-five years after the event] but some are fallen asleep. After that He was seen of James, then of all the Apostles, and last of all He was seen of me also." (1 Cor. xv. 1.)

If the reader compares this with the accounts in any one of the Four, he will find that it gives the fullest list of our Lord's appearances which has come down to us, and this, be it remembered, forming part of the most categorical declaration of what the Gospel is, to be found in the New Testament.[1]

---

[1] One is in amazement when one reads, in the work of a man who professes to have such a love of truth, the words, " The fact is, that we have absolutely no contemporaneous history at all as to what the first promulgators of Christianity actually asserted" (vol. i. p. 193). This writer, as far as I remember, gives us no reason to believe that he doubts the authenticity of St. Paul's earlier Epistles. Again, what is " contemporary history ?" Surely, if a man was now to write the history of the Crimean war in 1854-5, it would be a contemporary history.

A man, then, writes in A.D. 57 or earlier, that another Who had died in A.D. 32 had been seen by a number of persons, and among these, by 500 persons at once, of whom the greater part were alive when he wrote, and implying that the story had been believed ever since, and received by him (the writer) from those who had seen this Jesus, and that the fact was so essential to the religion that it was itself called "the Gospel," a name continually given to the whole system of Christianity, and moreover that he himself, when in company with others, had seen this Jesus at noon-day, and, the history asserts, had been blinded by the sight. Now let the reader recall to his mind any public man who died twenty-five years ago, that is, in 1850, and imagine this man appearing, not as a disembodied spirit, but in his resuscitated body to first one of his friends, then to eleven or twelve, then to another, then to five hundred persons at one time, and a flourishing and aggressive institution founded upon this his appearance, and numbers of persons giving up their property, and breaking with all their friends, and adopting a new religion, and a new course of life of great self-denial, and even encountering bitter persecution and death, simply because they believed this man to be alive from the dead, and moreover some professing to do miracles, and to confer the power of doing miracles in the name and by the power of this risen man.

Let the reader, I say, try to imagine all this, and then he will be able to judge of the credulity with which the author credits his readers when he writes:—

"All history shows how rapidly pious memory exaggerates and idealizes the traditions of the past, and simple actions might readily be transformed into miracles as the narrative circulated, in a period so prone to superstition, and so characterized by love of the marvellous." (Vol. ii. p. 209.)

" All history," the author says; but why does he not give us a few instances out of " all history," that we might compare them with this Gospel account, and see if there was anything like it?

Such a story, if false, is not a myth. A myth is the slow growth of falsehood through long ages, and this story of the Resurrection was written circumstantially within twenty years of its promulgation, by one who had been an unbeliever, and who had conferred with those who must have been the original promoters of the falsehood, if it be one.

To call such a story a myth, is simply to shirk the odium of calling it by its right name, or more probably to avoid having to meet the astounding historical difficulty of supposing that men endured what the Apostles endured for what they must have known to have been a falsehood, and the still more astounding difficulty that One Whom the author of "Supernatural Religion" allows to have been a Teacher Who "carried morality to the sublimest point attained or even attainable by humanity," and Whose " life, as far as we can estimate it, was uniformly noble and consistent with his lofty principles," should have impressed a character of such deep-rooted fraud and falsehood on His most intimate friends.

The author of " Supernatural Religion" has, however, added another to the many proofs of the truth of the Gospel. In his elaborate book of 1,000 pages of attack on the authenticity of the Evangelists he has shown, with a clearness which, I think, has never been before realized, the great fact that from the first there has been but one account of Jesus Christ. In the writings of heathens, of Jews, of heretics,[1] in lost gospels, in contemporary accounts, in the earliest traditions of the Church, there appears but one account, the account called by its first proclaimers the Gospel; and the only explanation of the existence of this Gospel is its truth.

---

[1] Celsus, for instance, who had been some time dead when Origen refuted him, knew no other account than the one which he calumniated; Josephus the Jew knew no other, Trypho suggests no counter story. The wild exaggerations of the heretics refuted by Irenæus all presupposed the one narrative, and can have had no other basis.

THE END.

CHISWICK PRESS:—PRINTED BY WHITTINGHAM AND WILKINS, TOOKS COURT, CHANCERY LANE.

THEOLOGICAL WORKS

PUBLISHED BY

GEORGE BELL & SONS.

BARRETT (A. C.) Companion to the Greek Testament. For the use of Theological Students and the Upper Forms in Schools. By A. C. Barrett, M.A., Caius College. *Third edition, enlarged and improved.* Fcap. 8vo. 5s.

This volume gives in a condensed form a large amount of information on the Text, Language, Geography, and Archæology; it discusses the alleged contradictions of the New Testament and the disputed quotations from the old, and contains introductions to the separate books.

BARRY (Dr.) Notes on the Catechism. For the Use of Schools. By the Rev. Alfred Barry, D.D., Principal of King's College, London. *Second edition, revised.* Fcap. 2s.

BLENCOWE (E.) Plain Sermons by the Rev. E. Blencowe. Vol. I. *Sixth edition.* Fcap. 8vo. 6s.

BLUNT (J. S.) Readings on the Morning and Evening Prayer and the Litany. By J. S. Blunt. *Third edition.* Fcap. 8vo. 3s. 6d.

—— Life after Confirmation. 18mo. 1s.

BOYCE (E. J.) Examination Papers on Religious Instruction. By Rev. E. J. Boyce, M.A. Sewed. 1s. 6d.

—— Catechetical Hints and Helps. A Manual for Parents and Teachers on giving Instruction to Young Children in the Catechism of the Church of England. *Second edition.* Fcap. 2s.

BUTLER (Bp.) Sermons and Remains. With Memoir by the Rev. E. Steere, LL.D., Missionary Bishop in Central Africa. 6s.

⁎ This volume contains some additional remains, which are copyright, and render it the most complete edition extant.

—— Three Sermons on Human Nature, and Dissertation on Virtue. Edited by W. Whewell, D.D. With a Preface and a Syllabus of the Work. *Fourth and cheaper edition.* Fcap. 8vo. 2s. 6d.

CARTER (T. T.) The Devout Christian's Help to Meditation on the Life of Our Lord Jesus Christ. Containing Meditations and Prayers for every day in the year. Edited by the Rev. T. T. Carter, Rector of Clewer. 2 vols. Fcap. 8vo. 12s. Or in five parts, three at 2s. 6d.; and two at 2s. each.

COMPTON (B.) Private Devotions for Church Helpers. By the Rev. B. Compton, Rector of All Saints', Margaret Street. 16mo. Cloth. 1s. 6d.

DAVIES (T. L. O.) Bible-English. Chapters on Words and Phrases in the Authorized Version of the Holy Scriptures and the Book of Common Prayer, no longer in common use; illustrated from contemporaneous writers. By the Rev. T. Lewis O. Davies, M.A., Vicar of St. Mary-extra, Southampton. Small crown 8vo. [*In the press.*

DENTON (W.) A Commentary on the Gospels for the Sundays and other Holy Days of the Christian Year. By the Rev. W. Denton, A.M., Worcester College, Oxford, and Incumbent of St. Bartholomew's, Cripplegate. Vol. I. Advent to Easter. *Third edition.* 18s. Vol. II. Easter to the Sixteenth Sunday after Trinity. *Second edition.* 18s. Vol. III. Seventeenth Sunday after Trinity to Advent; and Holy Days. *Second edition.* 18s.

—— Commentary on the Epistles for the Sundays and other Holy Days of the Christian Year. By the Rev. W. Denton, Author of 'A Commentary on the Gospels,' &c. Vol. I. Advent to Trinity. 8vo. *Second edition.* 18s. Vol. II. Completing the work. 18s.

DENTON (W.) A Commentary on the Acts of the Apostles. Vol. I. 18s. Vol. II. *preparing.*

These Commentaries originated in Notes collected by the compiler to aid in the composition of expository sermons. They are derived from all available sources, and especially from the wide but little-known field of theological comment found in the 'Schoolmen' of the Middle Ages. The special nature of the sources from which they have been derived ought to make them indispensable to all who wish to expound the Holy Scriptures with as much understanding as may be obtained by extraneous help.

—— The Grace of the Ministry. Considered as a Divine Gift of uninterrupted Transmission and Twofold Character. Edited by the Rev. William Denton, M.A. Oxon., Author of 'Commentary on the Gospels and Epistles,' &c. 8vo. 16s.

GOODWIN (Bp.) Confirmation Day. Being a Book of Instruction for Young Persons how they ought to spend that solemn day. By the Right Rev. Harvey Goodwin, D.D., Bishop of Carlisle. Eighth Thousand. 2d., or 25 for 3s. 6d.

—— Plain Sermons on Ordination and the Ministry of the Church. Preached on divers occasions by Harvey Goodwin, D.D. Crown 8vo. 6s.

'The suggestions offered in these pages are all in good taste, and inspired by a true regard for the interests of the Church.'—*English Churchman.*

'Very simple in their teaching, direct, unadorned, and not doctrinal.'— *Literary Churchman.*

—— Parish Sermons. By Harvey Goodwin, D.D. First Series. *Third edition.* 12mo. 6s. Second Series (*Out of print*). Third Series Third edition. 12mo. 7s. Fourth Series, 12mo. 7s. With Preface on Sermons and Sermon Writing. 7s.

—— A Guide to the Parish Church. By Harvey Goodwin, D.D. 1s. sewed; 1s. 6d. cloth.

—— Lectures upon the Church Catechism. By Harvey Goodwin, D.D. 12mo. 4s.

—— Sermons Preached before the Universities of Oxford and Cambridge. By Harvey Goodwin, D.D. [*In the press.*

—— Plain Thoughts concerning the Meaning of Holy Baptism. By Harvey Goodwin, D.D. *Second edition.* 2d., or 25 for 3s. 6d.

GOODWIN (Bp.) The Worthy Communicant; or, 'Who may come to the Supper of the Lord?' By Harvey Goodwin, D.D. *Second edition.* 2d., or 25 for 3s. 6d.

HARDWICK (C. H.) History of the Articles of Religion. To which is added a Series of Documents from A.D. 1536 to A.D. 1615. Together with illustrations from contemporary sources. By the late Charles Hardwick, B.D., Archdeacon of Ely. *Second edition, corrected and enlarged.* 8vo. 12s.

HAWKINS (Canon). Family Prayers :—Containing Psalms, Lessons, and Prayers, for every Morning and Evening in the Week. By the late Rev. Ernest Hawkins, B.D., Prebendary of St. Paul's. *Fourteenth edition.* Fcap. 8vo. 1s.

HOOK (W. F.) Short Meditations for Every Day in the Year. By the Very Rev. W. F. Hook, D.D., Dean of Chichester. *New edition, carefully revised.* 2 vols. Fcap. 8vo. Large type. 14s. Also 2 vols. (1260 pages). 32mo. Cloth, 5s.; calf, gilt edges, 9s.

—— The Christian Taught by the Church's Services. *A new edition, revised and altered to accord with the New Lectionary.* 1 vol. Fcap. 8vo. Large type. 6s. 6d. Also 1 vol. (490 pages). Royal 32mo. Cloth, 2s. 6d.; calf, gilt edges, 4s. 6d.

—— Holy Thoughts and Prayers, arranged for Daily Use on each Day of the Week, according to the stated Hours of Prayer. *Fifth edition, with additions.* 16mo. Cloth, red edges, 2s.; calf, gilt edges, 3s.

—— Verses for Holy Seasons. By C. F. Alexander. Edited by the Very Rev. W. F. Hook, D.D. *Fifth edition.* Fcap. 3s. 6d.

HUMPHRY (W. G.) An Historical and Explanatory Treatise on the Book of Common Prayer. By W. G. Humphry, B.D., late Fellow of Trinity College, Cambridge, Prebendary of St. Paul's and Vicar of St. Martin-in-the-Fields. *Fifth edition, revised and enlarged.* Fcap. 8vo. 4s. 6d.

—— The New Table of Lessons Explained, with the Table of Lessons and a Tabular Comparison of the Old and New Proper Lessons for Sundays and Holy Days. By W. G. Humphry, B.D. Fcap. 1s. 6d.

LEWIN (T.) The Life and Epistles of St. Paul. By Thomas Lewin, Esq., M.A., F.S.A., Trinity College, Oxford, Barrister-at-Law, Author of ' Fasti Sacri,' ' Siege of Jerusalem,' ' Cæsar's Invasion,' ' Treatise on Trusts,' &c. With upwards of 350 Illustrations finely engraved on Wood ; Maps, Plans, &c. In 2 vols. *Third edition, revised.* Demy 4to. 2*l.* 2*s.*

—— Fasti Sacri ; or, a Key to the Chronology of the New Testament. 4to. 21*s.*

LIAS (J. J.) The Doctrinal System of St. John, considered as evidence for the date of his Gospel. By the Rev. J. J. Lias, M.A., Professor of Modern Literature and Lecturer on Hebrew at St. David's College, Lampeter, sometime Scholar of Emmanuel College, Cambridge. Cr. 8vo. [*Nearly ready.*

LUMBY (J. R.) History of the Creeds. By J. Rawson Lumby, M.A., Tyrwhitt's Hebrew Scholar, Crosse Divinity Scholar, Classical Lecturer of Queens', and late Fellow of Magdalene College, Cambridge. Crown 8vo. 7*s.* 6*d.*

—— The Ancient Confessions of the Sixteenth Century, with special reference to the Articles of the Church of England. By J. Rawson Lumby. [*In the press.*

MILL (Dr.) Lectures on the Catechism. Delivered in the Parish Church of Brasted, in the Diocese of Canterbury. By W. H. Mill, D.D., formerly Regius Professor of Hebrew in the University of Cambridge. Edited by the Rev. B. Webb, M.A. Fcap. 8vo. 6*s.* 6*d.*

—— Observations on the attempted Application of Pantheistic Principles to the Theory and Historic Criticism of the Gospels. By W. H. Mill, D.D. *Second edition, with the Author's latest notes and additions.* Edited by his Son-in-law, the Rev. B. Webb, M.A. 8vo. 14*s.*

—— Five Sermons on the Temptation of Christ our Lord in the Wilderness. Preached before the University of Cambridge in Lent, 1844. By W. H. Mill, D.D. *New edition.* 8vo. 6*s.*

MONSELL (Dr.) Simon the Cyrenian, and other Poems. *Second Thousand.* 32mo. 5*s.*

—— Watches by the Cross. *Second edition.* Cloth, red edges, 1*s.*

—— Our New Vicar ; or, Plain Words about Ritual and Parish Work. Fcap. 8vo. *Seventh edition.* 5*s.*

—— The Parish Hymnal ; after the Order of the Book of Common Prayer. Cloth, 32mo. 1*s.* 4*d.*

MONSELL (Dr.) Hymns of Love and Praise for the Church's Year. By the late Rev. J. S. B. Monsell, LL.D., Vicar of St. Nicholas, Guildford. *Second edition.* Fcap. 8vo. 3*s.* 6*d.*

—— The Winton Church Catechist. Questions and Answers on the Teaching of the Church Catechism. 32mo. cloth, 3*s.* Also in Four Parts, 6*d.* or 9*d.* each.

PAPERS on Preaching and Public Speaking. By a Wykehamist. *Second thousand.* Fcap. 8vo. 5*s.*

PARISH PRIEST'S (The) Book of Offices and Instructions for the Sick. Compiled by a Priest of the Diocese of Sarum. Post 8vo. 3*s.* 6*d.*

PEARSON (Bp.) on the Creed. Carefully printed from an Early Edition. With Analysis and Index. Edited by E. Walford, M.A. Post 8vo. 5*s.*

PEROWNE (Canon). The Book of Psalms; a New Translation, with Introductions and Notes, Critical and Explanatory. By the Rev. J. J. Stewart Perowne, B.D., Canon Residentiary of Llandaff, Fellow of Trinity College, and Hulsean Professor of Divinity, Cambridge. 8vo. *Third edition.* Vol. I. 18*s.* Vol. II. 16*s.*

—— The Book of Psalms. An abridged Edition for Schools and Private Students. Crown 8vo. 10*s.* 6*d.*

—— Immortality. Four Sermons preached before the University of Cambridge. Being the Hulsean Lectures for 1868. By J. J. S Perowne, B D., Canon of Llandaff, Vice-Principal and Professor of Hebrew in St. David's College, Lampeter. 8vo. 7*s.* 6*d.*

PINNOCK (W. H.) Christ our King. A Narrative of His Life and Ministry, and of the Foundation of His Kingdom. By the Rev. W. H. PINNOCK, LL.D., Corpus Christi College, Cambridge, Author of 'Clerical Papers,' &c. Demy 8vo. *[Immediately.*

SADLER (M. F.) The Church Teacher's Manual of Christian Instruction. Being the Church Catechism expanded and explained in Question and Answer, for the use of Clergymen, Parents and Teachers. By the Rev. M. F. Sadler, Author of 'Church Doctrine—Bible Truth,' 'The Sacrament of Responsibility,' &c. *Twelfth thousand.* Fcap. 8vo. 2*s.* 6*d.*

'It is impossible to overrate the service to religious instruction achieved by this compact and yet pregnant volume . . . . We owe many boons to Mr. Sadler, whose sermons and theological lectures and treatises have wrought much good in matters of faith This Catechetical Manual is second to none of such.'—*English Churchman.*

SADLER (M. F.) The One Offering. A Treatise on the Sacrificial Nature of the Eucharist. Fcap. *Second edition.* 2s. 6d.

—— The Second Adam and the New Birth; or, the Doctrine of Baptism as contained in Holy Scripture. *Fourth edition, greatly enlarged.* Fcap. 8vo. 4s. 6d.

> 'The most striking peculiarity of this useful little work is that its author argues almost exclusively from the Bible. We commend it most earnestly to clergy and laity, as containing in a small compass, and at a trifling cost, a body of sound and Scriptural doctrine respecting the New Birth, which cannot be too widely circulated.'—*Guardian.*

—— The Sacrament of Responsibility; or, Testimony of the Scripture to the Teaching of the Church on Holy Baptism, with especial reference to the Cases of Infants; and Answers to Objections. *Sixth edition.* 6d.

—— The Sacrament of Responsibility. With the addition of an Introduction, in which the religious speculations of the last twenty years are considered in their bearings on the Church doctrine of Holy Baptism, and an Appendix giving the testimony of writers of all ages and schools of thought in the Church. On fine paper, and neatly bound in cloth. 2s. 6d.

—— Church Doctrine—Bible Truth. *Tenth thousand.* Fcap. 8vo. 3s. 6d.

> This work contains a full discussion of the so-called Damnatory Clauses of the Athanasian Creed. The new edition has additional Notes on Transubstantiation and Apostolical Succession.
>
> 'Some writers have the gift of speaking the right word at the right time, and the Rev. M. F. Sadler is pre-eminently one of them. 'Church Doctrine —Bible Truth,' is full of wholesome truths fit for these times. · · · · · He has the power of putting his meaning in a forcible and intelligible way, which will, we trust, enable his valuable work to effect that which it is well calculated to effect, viz. to meet with an appropriate and crushing reply one of the most dangerous misbeliefs of the time. —*Guardian.*

—— Parish Sermons. Trinity to Advent. *Second edition.* 6s.

—— Plain Speaking on Deep Truths. *Third edition.* 6s.

—— Abundant Life, and other Sermons. 6s.

—— Scripture Truths, A Series of Ten Tracts on Holy Baptism, The Holy Communion, Ordination, &c. Prices ½d. 1d., or 1½d. according to size.

SADLER (M. F.) The Communicant's Manual; being a Book of Self-examination, Prayer, Praise, and Thanksgiving. By the Rev. M. F. Sadler. Royal 32mo. *Sixth thousand.* Roan, 2*s.*; cloth, 1*s.* 6*d.* Also in best morocco, 7*s.*

*** A Cheap Edition in limp cloth. *Sixteenth thousand.* 8*d.*

―― A Larger Edition on fine paper, red rubrics. Fcap. 8vo. 2*s.* 6*d.* ; best morocco, 8*s.* 6*d.*

SCRIVENER (Dr.) Novum Testamentum Græcum, Textus Stephanici, 1550. Accedunt variæ lectiones editionum Bezæ, Elzeviri, Lachmanni, Tischendorfii, et Tregellesii. Curante F. H. Scrivener, M.A., LL.D. 16mo. 4*s.* 6*d.*

This Edition embodies all the readings of Tregelles, and of Tischendorf's Eighth or latest Editions.
An Edition with wide Margin for Notes. 7*s.* 6*d.*

―― Codex Bezæ Cantabrigiensis. Edited, with Prolegomena, Notes, and Facsimiles, by F. H. Scrivener, M.A., LL.D., Prebendary of Exeter. 4to. 26*s.*

―― A Full Collation of the Codex Sinaiticus with the Received Text of the New Testament; to which is prefixed a Critical Introduction. By F. H. Scrivener, M.A. *Second edition, revised.* Fcap. 8vo. 5*s.*

―― A Plain Introduction to the Criticism of the New Testament. With forty Facsimiles from Ancient Manuscripts. Containing also an Account of the Egyptian Versions by Canon Lightfoot, D.D. For the Use of Biblical Students. By F. H. Scrivener, M.A., Trinity College, Cambridge. *New edition.* Demy 8vo. 16*s.*

―― Six Lectures on the Text of the New Testament and the ancient Manuscripts which contain it. Chiefly addressed to those who do not read Greek. By the Rev. F. H. Scrivener. With facsimiles from MSS. &c. Crown 8vo. 6*s.*

THOMAS À KEMPIS. On the Imitation of Christ. A New Translation. By H. Goodwin, D.D. *Third edition.* With fine Steel Engraving after Guido, 5*s.*; without the Engraving, 3*s.* 6*d.* Cheap edition, 1*s.* cloth ; 6*d.* sewed.

YOUNG (Rev. P.) Daily Readings for a Year, on the Life of Our Lord and Saviour Jesus Christ. By the Rev. Peter Young, M.A. *Third edition, revised.* 2 vols. 8vo. 1*l.* 1*s.*